Sarah Ulmer

illustrations by Lisa Conn

All rights reserved.

Copyright ©2007 by Sarah R. Ulmer

Illustrations by Lisa Conn

ISBN: 978-0-9792780-7-5

Published and distributed by:
High-Pitched Hum Publishing
321 15th Street North
Jacksonville Beach, FL 32250

www.highpitchedhum.net

No part of this book may be reproduced or transmitted in any form or means, electronic or mechanical, including photocopying, recording, or by any information storage and retrieval system, without permission in writing from the publisher.

I Can Tap Dance and be are registered trademarks of be publishing, inc.

This book is dedicated to the boy who punched me in the stomach in the seventh grade, drew funny pictures of me on the blackboard, and told me I was too skinny ... wherever you are.

CONTENTS

Introduction i

WARNING v

Chapter One	Coloring Outside the Lines	1
Chapter Two	Tessie the Tap Dancing Orphan	17
Chapter Three	The Stick Figure	39
Chapter Four	Look Through Your Good Eye	53
Chapter Five	Almost Killed in the Cold Dip	71
Chapter Six	Stop and Watch the Lilies	95
Chapter Seven	Henry the Rat	131
Chapter Eight	Don't Flush the Toilet, ...	151
Chapter Nine	Sleeping With the Enemy	167
Chapter Ten	Don't Throw Darts	189

Chapter Eleven	STOP! Hammer Time	221
Chapter Twelve	Lamp, not Spotlight	243
Chapter Thirteen	Botox Gives You Amnesia	265
Chapter Fourteen	God is in the Pizza	287
Chapter Fifteen	Stairway to Heaven	311
Chapter Sixteen	Tessie Strikes Back	353
Chapter Seventeen	Hasta Luego	375

Justbeopen.com   387

Q: Will this book change my life?

magic eight ball

The Hook

Otherwise known as the Introduction.

Has anyone ever said any of these words to you?

- How can you say, "I love me," and not feel as if you are better than everyone else?
- How are you happy all the time?
- I would be happy if I had your body.
- I wish I could be more like _____ (insert attractive famous person here).
- I wish I had your ____ (insert random material possession here).
- You are inspiring, wise and real.
- You are different from anyone I know.
- You are enlightened. You really helped me.
- I want to be pretty. I want to *feel* pretty.
- Your energy is contagious. I love being around you.
- You should be a teacher.
- You have a strong message women need to hear.
- You are a good kisser (I threw that one in because it made me feel good to write it).
- **You should write a book.**

They have been said to me.

Now, a good friend of mine just brought to my attention that there is a fine line between sounding arrogant and being confident. I do not want you to have a poor impression of me right off the bat. She said you do not know me; you are not aware I am not arrogant. You have not read the book and simply do not know all the weaknesses we will discuss.

The point is, I want to tell you how I came to hear only the very positive words people say about me and make a choice to believe these positive statements. I mean, I suppose I could have written all the negative things people say to me or about me, but then, what would be the point of this book? If I dwelled on the negative well then, I would not be so darned happy all the time, now would I?

I once heard this statement ...and to whoever said it first, I would acknowledge you but I do not know who you are...

"What people think of me is none of MY business."

It has taken 33 years and many, and I mean many, experiences and pains for me to believe that statement. But, yes, I am 33 years old and I am 100% comfortable in my own skin. I know the reason I am alive. I know who I am. I love my life. I love myself, "flaws" included. I simply live life.

I am neither a PhD nor a therapist. I do not have my own TV show. I am not a multimillionaire. I do not even know if I am wise. **I am just a regular person with a message, just like you.**

But, you want to know how I am confident and do not live the life of insecurity that seems to plague many women—heck, most people? **How I can walk around *not* feeling empty inside? How I can say my life has a wonderful purpose and I actually *know* what it is?**

Let's make a deal:

> Allow me a chance to tell you my story and you can decide if it is confidence or arrogance. I am pretty sure you might laugh along the way and even leak a few tears. I would like to believe you will learn something and walk away with tools to build your own confidence, message and purpose for your life. **But I think I have to start at the beginning...**

You coming?

WARNING

I will mention God in this book. GASP!
Now, if that bothers you, you can either:

A: not read any further
B: realize that my liking this cool guy, God, is not meant to offend you

Actually, I think He is genderless. So, if you think "He" should be "She," that is okay by me. He is both. It's just easier to pick one gender, when writing, like boats. They are "she." Knock yourself out. You may substitute the word "God" for anything making it more personal to you. You may cross it out altogether.

Use the following suggestions if you like:
Source, Higher Power, Universe, Mother Earth, Energy, Vibration, Inner Voice, Conscience, Allah, Buddha, Yourself, Spirit, The Great Being, Creator, Your Dog, _____
(insert your own here).

I do not care how you relate the figure of "God," just relate. I have friends who are agnostics, Christians, Jews, Muslims, atheists, Buddhists, Kabbalists, Catholics, Seventh-day Adventists, Confused-ians (my made-up word for my confused friends), etc. I do not have a Scientologist friend. So, if you care to volunteer and show me how we can relate, write me. Maybe we can grab a cup-of-joe and chat.

Also, you will be asked to write, so you can either grab a pen and journal now, or just refuse—your choice. There is a fun exercise following each chapter called *Tool Time with Tessie.* **You might be surprised to discover the "writer" in you.**

You will be asked to speak out loud. Hey, it's fun. And if someone thinks you are talking to yourself, just say, "Yes. Yes, I am. Do you have a point?"

I will also introduce to you two characters—Tessie and George. I hope you come to love them as I do. Tessie represents an "unrecognized orphan" who found a voice. She is someone who also found the courage to step outside the box. I merely used the name Tessie to help tell my story. George represents the devil's advocate in all of us. He is my invisible friend. You, the reader, and I will both speak to him along the way. Feel free to take his side. You do not mind I have an invisible friend, do you?

Note: Although this is a true story, most names have been changed for various reasons.

I want you to know my plan is to keep this book as simple as possible. I realize I may use words normally not used while writing and I make a few grammatical errors. I even end sentences with a preposition. GASP! I allowed this for a reason. I would like you to have a bit of fun and not take the subject of mind, body and spirit so *seriously*, and find a way to relate to the message of this book. I think we can all agree there are enough books out there which intellectualize this very subject to the point of seeming "out of reach."

And in case of an emergency, please dial 911.

Now, on with the show.

Coloring Outside the Lines

Love your flaws.

They just might teach you something.

So, I am two years old. You didn't think I would go back that far, did you?

You are sitting there mumbling to yourself, "Man, this is gonna be a long one, George. She's going back like 31 years."

Well, yes, I have to go back to the beginning because **something significant happened to me at the tender age of two.**

I was always considered to be a perfectionist. Type A personality, they called it. That has been me ever since I could remember, ever since my parents could remember. My mother said she hated to ever punish me because I was just so hard on myself, it seemed redundant. I am pretty sure I used it to my advantage once or twice, maybe to get out of a spanking or two. Make the ole parents think I hated myself so bad for what I had done, so they would feel guilty about actually giving me one.

I wanted to do everything and anything by MYSELF! I did not need anyone's help. I tried anything new or exciting and I was thought of as a daredevil; the scarier, the better. I cannot believe, to this day, the only bone in my body ever broken is a toe. I remember I milked that for all it was worth. I think I wrapped it up for months and used crutches. It was my first broken bone—— very serious. It was not even my big toe.

Chapter One

So, here I am, two years old, 1975. My mom finally has a doctor confirm what she always knew from the day I was born——something was wrong with my right eye. My dad would argue with her those first two years. He even argued with the doctors. "She is beautiful. Her eyes are beautiful. She is perfect," he would say. My dad is also a perfectionist and pretty much thinks everything about me is amazing and wonderful. "I didn't say she was ugly," my mom would reply, "I said there is something wrong with her eye."

I have amblyopia. It is a condition most people know as a serious form of "lazy eye." In layman's terms——which are the only "terms" I know to speak——it means the brain does not "tell" the eye to see. Everything about my actual eye is in working order; everything is hooked up. All the parts are there but your brain "speaks" to your body and apparently it failed to "speak" to my right eye. Maybe that eye simply did not listen very well, which when you look at human nature, this is probably more likely the case. Either way, I was considered legally blind in that eye. It was as if I was in a dark room with merely a pinhole of light streaming in. I could see shadows pass by, but did not know what they were, how far away they were or see colors. That is what I see—or do not see—when I cover up my good eye.

So, what do you suppose the doctor told my parents to do? Put a patch over my *good* eye and make me walk around like that. Why would they do this to lil ole me, you ask? Apparently, if you cover up the good eye, it forces the brain to "speak" to the bad eye and give the SEE command. It basically retrains the brain to give that command and therefore, retrains the eye to really "listen." Then, to make matters worse, they would stick their finger in my bad eye and insert a hard contact lens. This was pre-soft contact days. Its purpose was to work together with the patch and strengthen the eye.

I think I lost about 13 contacts per year as I jumped off fences and ran into things. Remember, I have to do everything by myself. But you know what? My parents allowed me. If I said I could do it, then their response was, "Yes, you can"——and I did. So, at the age of two, I would stick my own little finger in my bad eye every day, insert a hard contact and put that patch over my good eye. My parents would wish me luck, spin me around three times, and send me out into the world. Here I was, walking around basically blind——on purpose——and I knew I was different.

Back in those days it was a pirate patch. I looked like the old, bald guy we all know, with the tattoo, who lost his eye in a war or something even cooler, like a robbery. I went into public like that. "Awww. What a cute little girl. Did you go to Long John Silver?" No, lady, I cannot see. My parents

Chapter One

did this to me because some man with bad breath and a weird, silvery light on his head told them to and now I bump into everything because I CAN'T SEE!!! I remember that, really. Only my doctor was actually a wonderful man, the best they say. The bad breath thing? Well, maybe I could be exaggerating a bit. I hear I have a tendency to do that.

Time passed and my parents discovered a different patch. No more Pirate Patch Sarah Bear. Now they had a flesh-colored type of patch that stuck onto the area around the eye and completely covered it. You have seen them on children, I am sure. It was harder to "cheat" with the new patch. I could not look under this one and I heard the comments: "What a shame. She is such a pretty, little girl."

Why was it a shame, exactly? I still felt pretty. My dad always told me I was. A girl needs her dad to tell her she is pretty. Did you know that? We will discuss that later. Anyway, I believed I was pretty, but I wanted to be pretty without shame.

So, my mom—my wonderful, insightful mom—she knew. She came up with the brilliant idea to paint my patch. I loved ladybugs and she transformed that patch into a beautiful ladybug.

Bondo

The patch represents our bondo. Needed for filling holes poked by others and by the "termites" of negative thought

   I thought she was a famous artist. I loved my new, one-of-a-kind, limited edition patch. Because I had to wear a new one every day, she painted a lot of them. I know the work that went into this process. Thank you, Mom.

Now, here is the important part. Are you ready? I felt different but I actually liked it, because being different was exciting. I received a lot of attention and questions and I *loved* the attention and loved to answer the questions. By simply telling others how the patch helped me, and how it was going to make my eye strong, actually made me strong. I was unique. They asked me if it bothered me. "No!" I would tell them, and I began to believe it, until it became a truth. My self-esteem grew from talking about it. That is true to this day. When I speak to people and tell them how to become strong, it creates strength in me.

My mom quoted the Bible. "You are fearfully and wonderfully made by God," she would tell me. I did not know at the time exactly what that meant, but I know I loved hearing it. I am different. I am one of a kind. I am a limited edition. I am pretty. I am strong minded. I can do anything. I am special. My parents love me and so does God. Life is good. I have a ladybug stuck to my face and you don't! I am very cool.

Chapter One

My poor parents. I walked the ridges of fences and walked into traffic with that patch on, and gave them heart attacks. I fell. I ran into things. I am surprised none of my teachers called social services to report them for all the bruises they must have noticed. I almost fell into a well once. My Uncle Ben literally saved me. I just could not be deterred from doing anything all by myself!

Why do I think this was important? Well, I am convinced the manner in which my parents handled my little type A personality and my "flaw," contributed in shaping my entire personality and self-esteem. Do I really think that one little success on their part did all of that? Yes, I do. There were more to follow, but at the age of two, trust me, it set a healthy pattern I now can see throughout my life.

Success!

They were handing me tools to put in my toolbox so I may pull them out when I need them. What am I building, you wonder? I am not going to tell you yet. We need to take this one step at a time. For now, I would like for you to go with me, through my life, and help me put tools in my toolbox. What we do with them is oh so important. I cannot wait to tell you——I get so excited thinking about it because it is the key to unlock this entire book. Oh, I am having so much fun by not telling you.

"She is kinda mean, George. I don't like secrets," you say.

Sledgehammer

Needed for tearing down. For now, hold onto it. We will have fun using it a bit later

I know you don't. Neither do I——unless I am the one with the secret. You just have to be patient. You too, George. Oh, is that a tool? Being patient. Maybe if you begin to read this book right here and now, thinking along those lines, you will figure out my secret. Let's see how smart you are. I will give you one tool right now: A sledgehammer. It is not for building, it is for tearing down. We are going to need it, so hold on to it.

Back to my parents. I can count several tools they have already given me. Go back and re-read the book, if you want. It is not that long. C'mon. For me? Tell me if you see any tools. If you cannot see them, I will help you in a moment. In fact, I have decided I will help you throughout each chapter. You can make it into a game, like the hidden picture. See if you can find them before I do. Hey, you might find some I did not mention, that would be great. Then you could write me and tell me. At the end of each chapter, we will have an optional exercise and recap session——*Tool Time with Tessie*. Got it? Good. Ok, now, back to the story.

In my opinion, my parents were genius. I see parents so often think they are "protecting" their children from "life."

Chapter One

They set unhealthy patterns for their little ones and are not even aware of what they are doing to them.

I see it at the playground.

"Mommy, can I climb up to the top of those monkey bars?"

"No, honey. You can't. You are not big enough. You could get hurt. Come down from there."

I saw it at a Paint-Your-Own-Pottery Studio.

"Mommy, do you think I can paint the eyes of my mermaid? It is hard, but I want them to be purple, and I want to paint her hair blue."

"No, honey. Eyes are not purple and that is a very tedious piece you have chosen. Here, let me do it for you. We wouldn't want to go outside the lines."

Jeez, lady. Since when is coloring "outside" the lines a bad thing? Did your mother tell you that?

My parents told me something so very different. "Yes, honey. You can do it. If you fall, get back up. We'll help you when you ask. If you go outside the lines, that's okay. Maybe going outside the lines will make us all see things a different way. Hair can be blue if you want it to. You are great. We will protect you from serious harm, but we will allow you to push your own limits, to define your own "lines." Show us what you can do. You are fearfully and wonderfully made." That is what I heard.

So, to answer one of those questions——"How can you say *I love me* and not feel as if you are better than everyone else?"——My parents did not need to put down any other children to make me feel better or love myself. They simply told me they believed in me. Subsequently I believed in myself and I came to love that patch. I loved being different. I was very cool. Go ahead, ask me about my imperfection. It is beautiful and even today I would not change it. I really wouldn't. A brain surgeon could walk up to me right now and tell me he could fix my eye, 100%, and I would refuse.

It did not work, by the way, the patch and hard contact, at least not the way the doctor had hoped. It worked for something entirely different. I was happy with myself, even with a "flaw." At the age of two, I loved *me*. Is that a success? I say, *yes*. Some people never have one day in their life where they can say, "I love me." Will their children see that and repeat the pattern? It is sad but it happens. We will talk about this very subject throughout the book, I promise.

Success !

Chapter One

I am now 33, and people can see my eyes are two different colors. They ask about it. I tell them and I still enjoy the questions. I still enjoy talking about it. They listen to my story and smile about the ladybugs——then I get them to help me judge the distance of my putts. He he.

My son, Caleb, is three. He asked me the other day if he could climb the monkey bars. I told him he could do it, then sat back and observed. He said he was a big boy and then added, "I can do it all by myself." Wonder where he got that? He defined his "lines," he went outside of them, asked for help when it became too overwhelming … and I was there. Even then, I kept repeating, "You can do it, Caleb." When he reached the top I told him, "You did it! Mommy is so proud of you. You're such a big boy. You did do it all by yourself."

Success!

Every night I tell him after he says his prayers, "You are fearfully and wonderfully made." I then add my own little verse.

"There is no one in the WHOLE wide world like Caleb, and I … love … you."

tool time with tessie

Oh, and I have to locate those tools correct? For now, just place them in your toolbox. We will use them as we move along and put it all together during Chapter 15. I promise. Ready? I gave you a **sledgehammer** and we found some **bondo**.

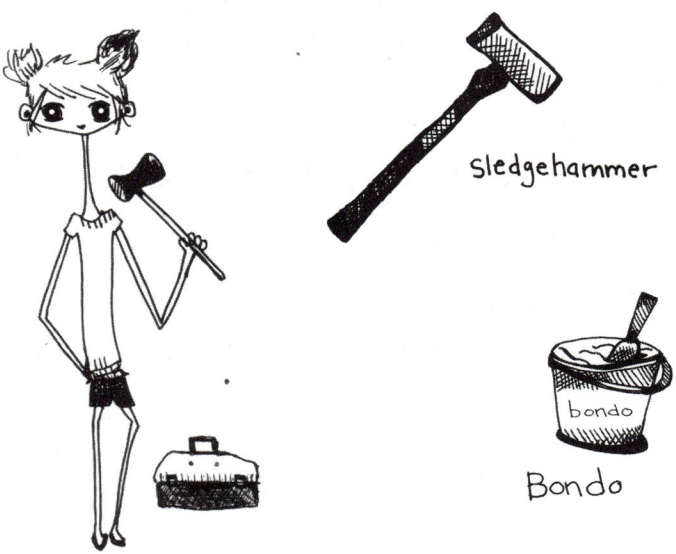

 Also, I want you to know we will be collecting **screws**.

The "spiritual lessons" we learn as we move along, are our screws. Screws hold the step together and our patterns must be secured with these lessons. I will be kind and give you ONE screw. There are many more, but you will need to take out your journal and find a few of your own. Again, you are not required to find them, but I am telling you, you are missing out if you don't.

So, what is one of our screws? Do you know? George?

 **WE ARE ALL THE SAME, BUT WE ARE ALL DIFFERENT AND *DIFFERENT IS GOOD***

Be Inspired.
Create.

> I love the lessons my creative mother taught me about thinking outside the box. I cannot thank her enough.

Why don't you take a moment to find your own "patch?"

What makes you unique?

Maybe you might be saying, "I don't love my flaws." Try writing. It certainly can't hurt. Maybe you paint or sing—— **find your own style of finding the love for you.**

Tessie the Tap Dancing Orphan

Erase fear by *allowing* yourself the opportunity to fail.

I remember the patch, but that is about all I remember from the age of two until about six or seven. You must be relieved, huh? I just skipped five years or so. For the rest, I rely on the stories of my parents.

When I entered my first potato sack race, I was determined to win. I must be the winner. Type A. Number one! ¡Numero uno! I could go on but I do not know any other languages.

It was a hot, sunny day, the day of the sack race. I was in the lead. I was going to win, I could feel it. I looked back at my second-rate competition and scoffed, "Ha! you——beat the likes of me? Ha!"——And then I fell. I sat there in shock, and cried like a big, big baby. I was not in pain, I only knew I did not want to be second. What was the point? What did second place do for you? Guess all that "pick yourself up and keep going" my parents tried to instill in me, did not take. I was second, or third or last. It did not matter, I wasn't first. So, I did not even finish. I sat there and cried and beat myself up for not winning. I shouldn't have looked back. Why did I look back? As I told you, my parents saw how hard I was on myself.

Man, that is tough. How do you find the happy medium between pushing your child and showing them how to have a little compassion for themselves when it is needed? Ease up, kid. You cannot always win. I just couldn't understand why not.

Chapter Two

Fast forward a bit to first grade. My mom picked me up from school one day, and I was crying——I mean, *crying*. I seemed to be in fear and torment; she could tell. She always made sure she was there to walk me home and listen to me and my amazing, blown out of proportion tales of the first grade. I discovered years later she napped all morning, while I attended school, just to find the energy to listen to me. Apparently, I was very passionate about everything and this had a tendency to exhaust her.

Anyway, where was I? Oh yes, I was crying and in sheer torment. She sat us both down on a bench and began her inquiry as to what made me so upset to cause me to be terrified to even speak. I mean, I was really afraid to tell her what I had done.

"You are going to spank me. Spank me really hard. I am a failure. I failed!" I sobbed.

She took a long breath and wondered what possibly could have been such a tragic failure, that I now obviously deserved to be beaten——hard, I might add.

"In what way did you fail?" she asked.

"I got an *F*. An *F*!" I wailed. Can you even get an *F* nowadays on anything in the first grade?

"What did you get an *F* in, Sarah?" my mom wondered.

"My spelling test," I cried. "Go ahead and spank me!" A first-grade spelling test had driven me to torment.

Now, if you are hoping for a dramatic account of how this prompted years of abuse by my mother and because of that, I have now found all of this insight as an adult and have relieved my tortured soul of all her control on me and my life——you will be very disappointed. Honestly, she sat there, exhausted from my over-exaggerated tale and hugged me.

I imagine her internal monologue went something like this: "What the heck? (my mom would never curse) What have I ever done to cause this little Sarah Bernhardt to even *think* I would give her a lashing, just for failing? For trying her best, and then receiving an *F*, on a first-grade spelling test, no less? Could you exhaust me any more than you already do? I need another nap."

So, after the hug, she told me she loved me even when I failed. I was not perfect (gasp!) and she never expected me to be. Failure was all a part of a learning process. It built character, like the sack race. She told me if I did my best, then she was proud of me. If I failed, or just flat out screwed-up, I

Chapter Two

could always feel safe in telling her. I do not think she liked the fact I was terrified to tell her about the *F.* I could tell her anything——*and she said <u>anything</u>*——and it would not change her love for me. She loved me as God did, unconditionally. I mean she made me feel that even if I broke all Ten Commandments at once, she would still love me.

I did feel safe. The "*F*," potato sack race and so many other lessons (I don't think you want to hear about all of the dramatic failures during my elementary years), those wonderful lessons, came to also shape me and my life. As a teenager, they became useful in helping me achieve and hold myself in high esteem. They did build my character and help create healthy patterns that would keep me out of "trouble." They aided me in trusting in my own power to make wise choices for myself. There is that word again——patterns. I have a feeling you will keep hearing it. Don't worry, we will get there. Be patient. But you will be disappointed, I was a very boring teenager. I did not even go into rehab for a drug problem nor did I pass out on our lawn after a night of binge drinking——or come home with strange piercings or tattoos, or get pregnant or anything. You will see. Boring.

power drill

Positive thoughts and messages are our drill. Drill them into your head

By the way, I never made an *F* on anything, ever again.

My mom stayed home with us during those formidable years. She was loving, tender, creative and she built us up. Us? Oh, I forgot, I have four siblings. They will be mentioned as we move along. Anyway, she made me feel as if I could do anything. I was invincible.

I think it was important she stayed home with us. I am not saying this is the way all mothers should do it or are able to do it, I am merely saying that is what she did and I love her for it. She always said if she stayed home with us and did not put us in day care, maybe when she was old and wearing Depends, we wouldn't put her in a nursing home. We will just have to see how she behaves over the next 20 years now, won't we? Really, that was a joke. Relax. My mom can live with me. She likes to do my laundry when she is here.

So, now I am about 10 or 11 and she decided we should be actresses. "We" means my sister Alison and me. We are only about 22 months apart, very close in age and spirit. We did fight a lot, though. She could be mean but I admit I provoked her. Yet, we loved each other and did about everything together. I will mention her now and then, so learn to love her.

Chapter Two

Makes sense, right? Being an actress, I mean. I was certainly passionate enough to be one and I was a perfectionist. I liked to dance, too. Why not acting? So, she spent all summer carting us to and from summer musical practice.

Annie was the play that year. I decided I was to become a star at the big theater downtown. All the schools in the county brought out their best talent and we auditioned for the roles. For four, glorious nights we were blessed to be able to perform, with a full orchestra, where all the traveling Broadway shows had stopped. Kindergarten through 12th grade, we all auditioned and had backdrops and sets from New York. Yes, I was to be a musical star!

Only one hitch. I could not sing. Here is where I say thank you to good ole Mom and Dad for not telling me I could do it—just this once—not telling me I could sing, that is. Otherwise you would be watching me on American Idol's "Best of the Worst Special." I mean, I am horrible. Just ask my junior high church choir director, he will tell you. We had a 300-voice choir and everyone was a member, including me. No one had to audition. He once stopped an a cappella arrangement, in frustration, and said, "Um, Miss Friese, do you think you could just mouth the words on this one?" Out of 300 people, he heard my horrible voice.

Oh well, make a joyful noise, is what the pastor said the Bible says. I was just making my noise. Jeez.

Okay, so we have now established the fact I cannot sing a note. Therefore, the role of Annie was out for me. How could I possibly be a musical star if I was not *the* star? How else could I stand out? Hhhmmmmm. Just then the director asked all of us kids, "Who amongst you has studied tap dancing?" Well, my arm shot up faster than a slippery hog at the fair. "I have studied tap dancing," I shouted.

I was now Tessie, the tap dancing orphan. I had three whole lines to speak, a tap dancing duet, but more importantly, I also had a solo. That means alone, by myself. The part was mine, all mine. I sold that director on my amazing tap dancing abilities because I... had studied tap.

My mother was in the back of the room and, you guessed it, she needed another nap. She pulled me aside. "Sarah, you don't know how to tap dance. How are you ever going to perform a tap dancing solo? Why did you tell her you could tap dance?" she asked with utter astonishment.

I peered back at her with equal astonishment. "Mom, she didn't ask *if* I could tap dance. She asked if I *studied* tap dancing, and I have studied it. I watch my friend Carey in tap dancing class like every week. If she can do it, well then, I'm sure I can!"

Chapter Two

Problem was, my mother knew I had a point. She built me up over the years to believe in myself and now, what could she tell me? She had to let me try, even if it meant I failed. I was just so excited and clueless to the fact that failing at this could cause me pain, therefore, I had no fear. I was Tessie, the tap dancing orphan. Now all I had to do was learn how to tap dance——minor detail.

My mom went home and took a nap. She always seemed to be napping now. Weird.

Self confidence
Believing in ourselves, prepares us for stepping outside the box *without* fear

She formulated our game plan, our plan of attack. We were poor. Did I mention that? Did you think just because she stayed home with us, we had money? Sorry. Nope. We were very poor, but she was even more creative——but we will get to that later. I will reserve an entire chapter just for her and her creativity. What about my dad? He was working hard for us. He was there, trust me. We will get to him, too.

Anyway, we were poor and that meant no money to buy tap shoes or tap lessons. So, she did what any broke, creative mother would do who could not say no to her daughter——she took me to a second-hand store, of course. Wouldn't you know it, a new pair of tap shoes sat there on the shelf in my size——with a ray of light shining on the price tag, which read $1.00. Honest, they were a dollar. Things always seemed to happen like that for us. We even bought a car once for a dollar. You can imagine what it looked like and I think it ended up burning my dad's leg or something, but we always seemed to have what we needed when we needed it. My mom said it was our faith in God, and I believed her. I loved God. He seemed to be really cool ——apart from the fact my dad ended up with a burnt leg and all.

So, I sat in my friend Carey's tap class, watched her and then went home and practiced in my basement what I had seen the teacher do. Shuffle Ball Change. Triple Time Step. Shuffle Ball Change. Buffalo. I did this all summer.

We sold tickets to the show and advertisements in the program. The prize for who could sell the most ads? An *Annie* sweat suit. My sister and I wanted to win. My mom did too. She was competitive and she liked to see us win. I think it made her feel as if she won as well, and if you think about it, she did.

She ushered us into the local retail stores and had us ask for the owner. We were to then give our little speech of why he or she should buy an ad in our professional program. I told

Chapter Two

them how I was Tessie, the tap dancing orphan. Alison was Duffy, the—well, she was Duffy. One of her lines was, "You are the Jack Dempsey of the orphanage," but she said, "Dack Jempsey," instead. She had to practice a lot. She did not get to tap dance. After all, only one of us could. We would tag team the owners and sell the heck out of the ads, and we heard "No" often. I hated hearing *no* but my mom would once again tell me failure built character and to go and try again. She was proud of us for merely trying.

You know what? Now that I think of it, now that I have owned a business——What was wrong with these people? Telling a cute little kid, "No, I won't support your dream." I mean, c'mon! We were kids in a local show. Support the local kids, you selfish @$$! (I was not allowed to curse. Not ladylike.) I mean, the ads were only between $15 and $100. Who were these guys? I wonder if they are still in business with an attitude like that.

To this day, I always buy something when a child has the courage to come up to me and ask. I stop by all the lemonade stands, encourage the kids and tell them how much I love that horrible lemonade. I do not even eat cookies, but each year I end up owning about 50 boxes of Girl Scout Cookies.

Nine times out of ten, I drop in when the local kids are

Encourage
Building someone else's confidence is rewarding

having car washes to raise money. You see them almost every Saturday in my town, holding signs to tell you they are going to cheerleading competition, in need of uniforms or trying to get to church camp. It does not matter what the sign says, it must be very important for those kids to stand out there on a Saturday, the day off of school, in the sun to wash my dirty car. I usually do not have time to even get the wash and simply wish them luck as I put money in the bucket. I relish the look on their faces when I tell them they do not need to wash my car to obtain my donation. Go live your dream, young man——young lady. I know how you feel. It is important for us to tell other children we believe in them. One can only hear it so many times from his/her own parents; it must be heard from outside sources. Remember that the next time they ask you to buy something. Okay?

Looking back, I think about that. But when you are 10 or 11, you just hear "no" and become sad. We learned quickly though, to gear up, because our mom would encourage us into another shop, one after another. We won those *Annie* sweat suits. In fact, we were in several musicals following *Annie* and won every year.

Chapter Two

We were proud and so were my parents.

So, it is finally opening night. Alison said, "Jack Dempsey," like a pro. Go, Duffy! I was proud of her because I knew how she struggled. I performed my tap dancing solo. Triple Time Step. Triple Time Step. Triple Time Step. Buffalo. Buffalo. Buffalo. Very impressive. I was on top of the world. Over a thousand people were there. Annie, Annie who? Pffffttt. Sure, she could sing, but I could tap dance. We did the same show four nights and I was sad when it ended. I now have the same feeling when a vacation has come to an end. It was over and I put away my tap shoes. I never used those shoes again, not those. I had done it. **I could tap dance.**

Success!

My poor parents. Can you imagine what they went through while I went to that basement every night? I mean, if I got up there and could not do it, no matter how much they believed in me, what would they tell me? It must have been hard for them to watch. I wonder how many conversations they had about whether or not to save me from myself. I think my dad used that expression a lot——"We have to save you from yourself." I wonder if he ever took naps.

How do you suppose I would have behaved if I humiliated myself in front of all those people and received an *F* in tap dancing? You saw what a first-grade spelling test did to me. I think, for my mom, a mere nap would not cover this one. I would have probably sent her into a five-year coma.

Once again let us imagine if they had handled it as many parents would have.

"Sarah, you just told a lie, a big lie. You cannot tap dance. You will embarrass yourself and you will embarrass us and you will embarrass your sister. Now, you march yourself down to that theater and tell that director you lied, young lady, before it is too late. Let a *real* dancer be Tessie, the tap dancing orphan."

But they did not do that, did they? I was determined to do it and they knew it. I did do it—very well, I might add. I am sure the choreographer knew, but she allowed me to keep up the pretense and brag about my tap dancing abilities. She never told anyone. Yes, I did it. I showed them all——but really, they showed me. They built me up. They encouraged me. They allowed me the opportunity to fail and that in itself was a success——another pattern. That word again, *pattern*.

Success!

Chapter Two

All of these small successes actually mean something. Do you see?

You do not need to be rich or famous to be considered a success. You are successful when you allow yourself even the *opportunity* to fail. You *must* allow yourself to fail in order to succeed.

I hope I am always like that little girl. No fear, just trying——believing in myself and forgetting the "no's"; keep moving until I find a "yes!" I can do anything if I put my mind to it and if other people put their minds to it, too. Because I now see those other people—my parents, the choreographer, the director—they also allowed me the opportunity to fail. They did not stop me, protect me or save me from myself or the failure. Do not listen to those proclaiming, "You are lying to yourself," when you say you can do something you have never tried before. If you believe you can tap dance, then do it.

Allow yourself the opportunity to fail,
you just might succeed.

November 16, 2006

Mom and Dad,

    I am 33 yrs. old, and yet I am still 3. Here I am wearing a patch on my eye and I'm telling you, "I can do it myself." If you stop by my house to check on me because you love me so much you hurt just by seeing me hurt, and would take all my pain if you could... well, you'll find me in here, on my bed, writing my attorney and texting my ex-husband and telling him where he can stick it... because, I can do it myself. I'm annoyed you stopped by unannounced. I don't need your help. I don't need your guidance or love or support or words of wisdom, because I can do it myself. I mean, you only had to take custody of my dog, because I can do it myself! Right?

    Why oh why would you ever think I needed your help? I mean, why would you stop by and check in on me? I am great, right? I am handling it all just fine, right? So fine I had to go on a trip, because I was crying so hard and didn't want my lil boy to think I had lost it. But I can do it myself. Right?

So, don't come over here and tell me you think I am special, and fearfully and wonderfully made, and God will get me through this, and you are here for me, and you would do anything for me. Don't baby me. No... that would be horrible parenting, right? I don't need it, right?

Ok. So I am about to fall into that well. I admit it. Please do not let me fall in. I am 3, walking around blind. I don't know where I'm going and I'm exhausting you by running into things, and by screaming about how I can do it all by myself. Do you need a nap, Mom? You wanna take a nap before I come home from school in tears and tell you how I made an "F" on my spelling test in life? How I "F'ed" up another marriage and, hopefully not, my kid? Do you need a nap? Have I exhausted you, once again, with my passionate cries and emotional, dramatic tears? I am sorry. I am still 3. I still have that patch on my eye.

Please keep loving me and telling me I am great and I can get through this. Please keep telling me you and God love me unconditionally and I am fearfully and wonderfully made. And I will get through this. Did I say that twice? Talk me through what I cannot see and guide me with your words. Please don't let me fall into the well. Please don't. And please know that I am really not 3, and I have learned and now see I never did it by myself. I think there were always a few people there helping, only they didn't always let me know it. For that I thank them. ... or should I say, thank you.

I love you and hope I can be even half the parent you are,

Sarah Bear

OOPS ...

Did I put that letter in there? I jumped ahead of myself. Well, that is called foreshadowing. I gave it away. My life has not always been so innocent and perfect, but I'm sure you already knew that. I was allowed many more opportunities to fail, more opportunities to tap dance. We will get there.

Chapter Two

My dear mother would like me to add something here. She is very honest—and I do mean, very.

She did not like the fact I said I went to the "basement" to practice my tap dancing. There aren't any basements in Florida, she says. We actually rented a three-story house and the ground floor was nothing but a garage and storage. The house did not even have an entrance until you reached the second floor, from the outside. So, I called it a basement. I am sorry I used the word "basement." I always thought it was and it just worked better for the story. It is better than, "I went down to the cold, wet, garage/storage space to practice." Better, Mom? Please don't take any more naps.

tool time with tessie

Hi! Did you like that story? I personally feel empowered after reading it. Now, gear up for our exercise. Put on your workout clothes if it makes you feel better. I also encourage you to go back and take a look at the illustrations. They may have a deeper meaning to you now as well.

What did we find for our toolbox?

power drill

Encourage drill bit

Self-confidence drill bit

We are getting somewhere. Aren't we?
Now all we need to do is screw in our affirmation.

 **FEAR DOES NOT STAND IN MY WAY**

Say it out loud and be proud.

Want a few more screws? Want to see yourself as a success? Take out your journal, tell your "tap dancing" story, and find your own affirmation to stamp out fear. I know you can.

Be Empowered.
Succeed.

The Stick Figure

Negative thoughts do not cause pain, *believing* them does.

So, the boy who punched me in the stomach and made fun of me. The thing is, we were actually friends, so do not be mad at him. We had one of those love/hate relationships. Maybe deep down I had a crush on him. Okay. I have thought it through and I did in fact have a crush on him. Man, I did not want to ever admit it.

I remember he was very cool and everyone liked him and his even cooler, older brother. They were football players. Remember when I said my sister could be mean, but I provoked her? Same principle applied to Ben. He punched me in the stomach one day, after a note I was passing fell into the hands of Mr. Heel, our Bible teacher. Irony.

Let's back up a bit before I get to the contents of the note. In the small, Christian school I attended, they broke us up into two classes. Ben was in one and I in the other. We had seven periods and seven different teachers with seven different subjects.

"George, she thinks we are stupid," you are thinking.

I do not think you are stupid. I just wanted to explain how we rotated classes. You might find I like to further explain things as we move along. This is not meant to insult you, George or your intelligence. Back to the story.

We rotated from one class to the next. I went to the room

Chapter Three

where Ben finished his class and vice versa. I cannot remember who started it first or why—— I am pretty sure it was him—— but we would draw caricatures of each other on the blackboard. I mean, HUGE pictures of one another and leave it for the arch enemy to find. The teachers did not know what we were drawing. Seriously, they didn't. They assumed we just liked to draw pictures on their blackboard. I know this because I went to a Christian school, and they did not condone making fun of one another or being cruel. I do not think we produced many Harvard grads, if you know what I mean.

So, I would walk into English class and find this picture on the board:

Notice the eyes are HUGE in comparison to the head, the bangs and feet prominent. The stick figure meant, well, just that——I was a skinny, skinny stick. Too skinny, big ugly hair, bug eyes and skis for feet. I will not draw how I portrayed him because this book is not about how my picture made him feel. Ben may write his own book or talk to a therapist about it. This is about what his picture did for me. Notice I did not say did *to me*, I said did *for me*.

I remember walking into chapel one day, and Ben was standing there holding two big, round offering plates up to his head. You know, the collection plates they pass in church? I could not even see his face. All I saw was hair, two big plates, neck, and then his body.

"Hello, everyone. Welcome to chapel. I am Sarah Friese and I will be your guest speaker," he proclaimed.

Yes, he was suggesting my eyes were huge. HUGE. Which they are. Jeez, kids. Can a sister get a break? You have been making fun of my eyes since I was two. I thought when I lost the patch, it would end. I think I was born with the eyes you curently see, only my head had to catch up. Seriously, they were as big as they are today, but were placed on my little kid head. I have now have discovered this is the case. Check it out. It is a scientific fact.

Everyone laughed, and I shook my head and made a mental

Chapter Three

note of his flat butt. I tried to imagine how I was going to master the feat of drawing him with a flat butt on the blackboard. To figure this out would take actual work and planning. How could I make his butt look flat, when I am not even skilled in the art of drawing three-dimensionally? I will get a book on how to do it. Yes, that is what I will do. There must be a book in the school library which will show me how to draw a flat butt on a human body. Oh, is chapel over? Did the pastor tell us something relevant or life altering? Guess my mind wandered there for a bit.

So, I was secretly planning my next picture of Mr. Flat Butt. Ironically, I have a very flat butt too. Weird. Anyway, I was planning this in a note to my friend Stephanie, when it was intercepted by Mr. Heel and he read it to the entire class. Ben heard about it and he punched me in the stomach when I came into the hallway. That was harsh, really. A brilliant plan ruined by Mr. Heel, and now I get punched. I tried to punch him back but he was swift. Dang football player.

hard hat

Protects our head from negative thoughts. Boy do I wish I would have acquired one earlier than I did!

Even though we did this to each other and neither of us seemed to be bothered by it, and we did not cry or act as if the teasing was hurting our pride in any way, I must now admit... the "skinny" part stuck.

Yup. That is right. I allowed it to creep into my head. I had always been told I was skinny, but this was the first time someone made it seem as if it was a bad thing. It stuck with me for many, many years.

Here is what we are going to discuss——Image and how allowing myself to think of that "flaw" in a negative way, unlike the patch, created many problems for me down the road. One negative thought hurt me. Well, let me say, *believing* that negative thought hurt me. Or did it? Confusing? It did hurt me but it also helped me. It has a happy ending.

I will also show you how I finally made a choice to begin to think of being skinny in a positive way. I mean, it took a while, but I did come back to the healthy pattern. You will learn how, just by changing that pattern of thinking, I changed my life. Me, falling into the trap of believing I was "too skinny," became the path—the entire path—which led me to several things. I am talking several, important things.

1. Discovering my passion. The whole reason God put me here. My reason for living. My gift to others. My message.

2. Discovering my career, which is also my message. How convenient for me.

3. Discovering who I am. Waking up every day, comfortable in my own skin. Loving myself. Not caring what others think. *Loving my flaws.*

Chapter Three

Yes, you heard right. This one simple thing—negative thinking about being skinny and changing that pattern to positive thinking about being skinny—led me to all of that. I mean, what I learned and the path I was to go down, they answer almost every question in "The Hook." It became my message and I want you to hear it:

You are beautiful.
No, you do not look like the aerobics instructor. You do not look like me. You do not have her body. You were not meant to. You have your body.

You are different.
You are not the movie star you so admire. You are not meant to be. You are you. You need to find the love for you. Quit trying to be someone else.

Do not envy me or her.
Do not get your hair cut like mine or hers. Do not envy my house or anything else I own or the Jones' house or anything they own.

Find your strength.
You are strong, too. You have something to say. Find your own voice, your own message. You have one. Speak it.

Your attitude is contagious.
You are happy. People want to be around you.

There is more...

> **You are a teacher.** Teach others.
> Teach your children. Tell people your message.
> Tell your children. Do not tell me you want my hair or body. You have your own and I bet it is much more beautiful than mine. If you cannot see that, you are not using the correct eye. Oh, you didn't know you have a third one? We will get to that.

You do not have to be famous to change lives.

Changing one life is a huge start.

Chapter Three

"How do I find my message?" asks George.

We will get there but the first step is to be still and look around you for a minute. Look outside the lines. Your message is there, you are not looking … or hearing. I am going to help you, do not worry. Sigh. I wish I had looked and heard a long time ago.

Okay, back on track. So, what happened to me? I explained to you how the patch and the way my parents handled it, created a love for me and my "flaws," right? That is true and I do love those flaws, all of them, *now*. It does not mean I didn't forget, now and then, when someone else came up to me with something negative to say. This is what I was trying to explain to you in "The Hook." I did not write all the negative things people have said to me. Today, I choose to remember the positive. I have learned how to make that choice, but this was another lesson I had yet to learn. Being conscious is much more difficult than it sounds.

Self love
Until you can love yourself, you cannot truly love another

I was not prepared for the other people who would come along. The ones who are so jealous or unhappy with themselves, they feel the need to tear others down. I had not seen that yet. My parents never tore me down. They did not teach me to be jealous. When I was two, I listened and gained my entire view of myself through my parents' eyes. As I grew, other people crept in and I *allowed* myself to be viewed in their eyes. Did you really get that? I *allowed* myself to be viewed in their eyes.

Remember the "*The Hook?*" "What others think of me is none of my business." Well, it took time to really believe it. So, do not judge me harshly and do not lose the lesson. That patch still created a strong love for myself, it just took me many years to think positively on the "too skinny flaw." The point is, I did come back to loving it and myself. I merely forgot for a while. I never said I was perfect and I was to learn a big lesson and my life would be changed because of it.

Success!

So, bear with me. I promise I will make sense of it all. I do not believe I can accomplish this with one chapter. We need to break it down step by step.

Chapter Three

"Oh no, George. She still thinks we are stupid," you cry.

I do not think you are stupid. I think you must be very intelligent if you are still reading my book (insert drum and cymbal sound here). I simply believe steps are easier to take than an entire staircase, so this is a short chapter.

You got off easy there, George.

tool time with tessie

A mere stick figure is teaching me about life. Amazing. I wonder what you have hidden in your life that could be teaching you. Did you allow someone else to establish your view of yourself? Maybe a magazine or movie?

Take the time to think about it.

Time to drop more tools in our toolbox.

We found a hard hat and another drill bit.

hard hat

Self love drill bit

Tessie's screw for the day is:

WHAT OTHERS THINK OF ME IS NONE OF MY BUSINESS

Say it with feeling until you capture the full meaning! I for one am tired of caring what others think of me.

Want more screws? You know the drill. Write. Draw pictures. Place your affirmations on self-stick notes on your mirror.

Be You. Shine.

Look Through Your Good Eye

Do not give your power away by allowing yourself to be viewed through someone else's eyes.

I was a pickpocket in *Oliver!* Yes, I told you I was in other musicals and this was the first one I was in. I was an afterthought, no big tap dancing lesson in this story. My older sister Shavaun was the one actually in *Oliver!* and I watched her rehearsals. I would sit in the audience as I developed a crush on the guy who played Fagan. I think his name was Brian and he was about 18. I was six.

It was my first crush and I liked to pretend I was pouting, over God only knows what, just so he would come over and ask what was wrong. When he saw me sitting there sulking, he would cheer me up by allowing me to sit on his lap. I liked to sit on his lap. I had a crush on him, remember? The pouting worked well for me and I used it as often as possible. I remember everyone figured this out and they laughed when I did it, but he always indulged me.

Soon everyone began to like me, I guess, and asked the director if I could be in the play. I was afraid to speak any lines but the cast thought I was so cute, they wanted me a part of the play. I was a mascot of sorts during rehearsals. Well, you guessed it, the director found a way for me to participate and not have any lines.

I was to be this little orphan who, during one musical number—the one where Fagan is teaching us how to pick pockets—would pick Fagan's pocket. I had the honor of pretending as if there was something in my eye. Big role.

Chapter Four

While Fagan looked into my eye, I pulled a gold watch out of his pocket without his knowledge. They specifically told me to cover my left eye and point out the problem to Fagan. My good eye, remember?

Well, this posed a problem because I kept missing his pocket and therefore I was not a very good pickpocket. They laughed a little, but then I stood on stage and explained to them all about how I could not see. I was a perfectionist and I wanted to do it exactly as the director instructed—cover up my left eye. The cast laughed and simply told me to cover the other one. It never occurred to me. A perfectionist always follows instructions.

Brian came over and gave me a kiss. From that moment on, I wanted to impress him. I now cared what he thought of me. This is my first memory of wanting to impress someone else— a man. Uh-oh, ladies. Not a very healthy beginning to a new pattern.

My mother was responsible for my costume. The secondhand store to the rescue. It was called "Nearly New" but my sister and I decided it should be called "Barely New." My mom was awesome. She found old, ugly clothes and somehow made them even uglier. I mean, I was a pickpocket, I lived on the streets. I was not supposed to be pretty. She sewed patches on an old vest and cut off pants to make the bottoms look ragged, found a pair of ancient, beaten-up shoes in my size. She created my costume and I hated it. I cried. I looked ugly. How could Brian love me if I looked ugly? At the age of six, I cared about what a man thought about my looks.

Self empowerment
Do not give your power away

My mom tried to break this pattern of thinking and told me it did not matter what anyone thought. Remember, I am fearfully and wonderfully made, just like the patch story? This time it did not work. I did not choose to accept it, my choice. I allowed myself to be viewed through someone else's eyes. I mean, give me a break. I was six. We all struggle with this one principle, all of us. I cried and refused to wear it.

Then, Brian heard I was not going to wear my costume. He came over and told me how cool it was and I was *supposed* to look ugly. It was acting. He explained how they made him look ugly for his part. My mom told me all of this but I chose to only listen to Brian. I wore it, **for Brian**. Not a very healthy pattern, huh?

Now we are back to "too skinny." Enter unhealthy pattern.

Chapter Four

Once again, I chose to listen to Ben and the ones who would follow him in saying I was too skinny. He actually did not mean it to be unkind, I do not believe. We enjoyed poking fun at one another and I hope he realizes I truly believe this. He will probably read this book. But others did intend to be cruel. Oh yes, there were more.

One girl stood in front of the class and said, "Sarah. Stand up."

I did.

"Turn sideways."

I did.

"Stick out your tongue."

I did.

"You look just like a zipper."

screwdriver

Others come along to shake our screws loose. We need a screwdriver of reassurance to tighten them back up

Hahahahahahahaha. All the kids laughed and so did I. I was compared to starving Ethiopians. Erin nicknamed me "Annie," short for anorexic. See, I would be Annie after all. I allowed her to call me that.

I even had a teacher come up to me at our formal banquet during my senior year in high school——the year when self-esteem is incredibly fragile.

"Sarah, you just look so anorexic tonight."

I mean, who was this woman? I went to the store, bought a dress, found a date, and spent hours getting dressed up, just so he would be attracted to me, and THIS is what you decided to say to me? On tonight of all nights? Thanks for the compliment, lady. You would think adults should know better. She probably chose not to break any of her own poor patterns and was continuing her behavior into adulthood. Wonder what she taught her daughter? Oh, we will get to that. I know exactly what she taught her.

Anyway, the point is, I began to believe I was too skinny. Don't you go blaming my parents, they fed me plenty. They kept repeating the fearfully and wonderfully made proverb, told me I was pretty. My dad reminded me over and over I was beautiful. He was a man. I did love to hear him say it. I still do. Girls need their daddies to tell them they are pretty. It is very important for the development of our self image. I, for the most part, believed I was attractive, but I was still a perfectionist and did not want to be too skinny. They reminded me I was not *too skinny* and explained these people were probably just jealous, and it was obvious they did not like themselves very much.

Chapter Four

Hearing what they told me did keep me from making fun of others, at least. I was not jealous of them. I loved myself. I did not want to hurt their feelings just so I would feel better. Some of the healthy patterns had taken hold, but I chose for them to. Ben is the only one I can remember I really picked on. After him, I decided to quit and I know I really did not do it before him either. It was not *me* and did not make me feel very good. I always stood up for the ones being tormented, never joined in the fun. My mother said she always admired this trait of mine. I went out of my way to befriend a little girl with braces on her legs. She was nice and the other kids picked on her. They quit when she became my friend.

Most of what my parents instilled in me, I chose to believe. I excelled in school, always on the honor roll. I was in National Honor Society, top of the class, and scored well on my SAT. I excelled in sports. I was a cheerleader. I was a leader and I am not bragging about those things in an unhealthy way. I am simply telling you I believed in myself. Those lessons my parents taught me, empowered me and I chose to put my best foot forward. They gave me confidence to *not* follow the crowd. Remember, I like being different. I wanted to stand out just as I did with the patch. So, I did not drink at all. I did not have sex. I said *no* to drugs.

I had strength to say *no* to those unhealthy things laid before me. We all feel peer pressure. You did and your children will. If someone made fun of me for being a virgin— and they did—I answered them with, "Yes. Yes, I am! What is wrong with that? And what is your point?" They did not have one. I stood there in my cheerleading skirt and they had nothing else to say. They dropped it and I never heard it again.

Cementing our patterns with belief is essential

Was I better than anyone else? Absolutely not. I was merely given the tools to make choices within my own power. My parents did not make them for me and I thank them for the tools they gave me. It was up to me to take them out of the toolbox and actually use them.

So, I did use them and I see another success. I resisted peer pressure and began to find myself. I established my own beliefs. I still loved me without putting anyone else down, without being cocky or arrogant. Did I ever become a little self-righteous? A little bit but mostly in my own mind. Do not worry, something major would happen to me and knock me flat on my @$$. Any amount of self-righteousness, which could have turned into a

Success!

Chapter Four

monster, was squashed out of me when I was about 22 years old. We will get to that.

If you are sitting there thinking, dangit, I did not do all of that, or maybe you did fall prey to peer pressure——maybe your kids are falling right this minute——do not panic. We have the sledgehammer, remember? We can talk more about image and peer pressure later if you want. It's a toughie.

I want you to take notice of one thing here, parents. We ALL worry our children will fall into trouble during the teenage years. I am not an expert you might admire, but notice I never said my parents were strict and because of these strict rules, I avoided trouble. I did not tell you I lived in fear to make straight A's, therefore I made them solely to avoid my parents' wrath. I did not say any of those things. I said they began giving me tools to use in my own power and they began handing me these tools at the age of two!

Now, I have explained I do not have a degree in child psychology, but maybe I can see my parents were on to something. By the way, Alison, the one to whom I am close in age, the one raised by both of them also ... she never wandered into trouble either. She excelled. Maybe my parents are the geniuses I keep telling you about. My parents do not need to influence one more life to be considered a success. They influenced ours. I say they are successful. I told them this when I was 18 years old. This time, my over-exaggerating manner in which I conveyed this to my mother did not prompt her to a nap. I pretty much remember it prompting her to tears.

Success!

We still need to get to the unhealthy pattern which was going to build my path and work its magic. Sorry. Felt I needed to take a side road there and lay some ground work for you to notice I was forming healthy patterns simultaneously.

So, what to do when you believe you are too skinny? Notice I will not admit I *am* too skinny, I just believed I was. This is an important point for you to file away as you read.

First, you need to know I gave my power away by believing these negative thoughts about myself. Next, what to do? Well, you eat, that's what. A LOT. In front of everyone. I ate and ate ... all the fattening, unhealthy stuff. I wanted to gain weight, then I would not be too skinny, right? I ate Whoppers from Burger King- double ones, milkshakes, fried chicken, ice cream. I did not even think about my health or what eating this way could do to me. I do not believe my parents knew how badly I ate when I was not at home. This pattern continued into my late twenties—— over-eating, eating poorly and harming my health along the way.

Chapter Four

Just because you are skinny, does not mean you are healthy. I developed cystic acne.

You thought I might have gotten something scarier than that, huh? Acne.

"What is the big deal? She did not develop anything life threatening. She was able to eat Whoppers and not get hips. I think she needs to shut her pie hole," George exclaims.

Hey, I will explain. Relax. Now, when you have this type of acne, cysts form under the skin and they are painful, I mean painful. I cried a lot. They woke me up at night when I turned over. They hurt more than just physically, they hurt my self-esteem a little. I mean, they were unattractive and they covered my cheeks and chin for all to see.

Here came the comments again: "What a shame. She is such a pretty girl."

Only this time, there were no ladybug patches for my mom to give me to cover it up.

I went to every dermatologist, took every type of medicine and wore every type of makeup. In fact, I would not leave the house without makeup. I kind of became obsessed and it made my daddy very sad. He still thought I was the most beautiful girl in school—in the whole world. He never quit saying it.

All the doctors told me one common thing: "It is absolutely not your diet. It is hormonal."

We will DEFINITELY get to this LIE later. Sorry, dermatologists everywhere, but I will have to go ahead and say it. I do not think you meant to lie to me, it is just what happened. Finding the truth to that lie led me to my current passion, my reason for being here. It was all a part of the path, my next step. We will get there.

So, I took all the medicines, slathered on all the cream——did not CURE the cysts, just kept them under control. How my mom and dad paid for it, I am not sure. I kept eating poorly and the cysts kept coming, just not as many, as I said. Now, when one of these cysts finally leaves——and it took weeks, even months for each one to leave——it erodes the collagen beneath the skin and leaves a scar, indentions on my face. That really stinks.

Now I *really* heard the comments: "What a shame. She is such a pretty girl."

They said it directly to me. I cried. People made sure to mention these scars. Why they felt the need to point them out, I will never know but I thank them now. They helped

Chapter Four

me climb more steps. I will now dedicate this chapter to them. Dedicate. There. Done.

I became obsessed with how to fix them. I tried dermabrasions, many of those. I even had a mini-facelift, because a surgeon told me if I let him CUT my face and nerves, he could stretch some of the scars out. I mean I let him cut me up for one reason: I was listening to others and allowing them to cause me to believe I was not pretty. The mini-facelift did help a little but the scars were still there, still are. A facelift——in my twenties.

My parents were not happy. They did not teach me this. My dad and mom kept telling me I was pretty, still very pretty. I was still fearfully and wonderfully made, smart, wonderful and unique. I was a limited edition. I was not listening. They kept to their patterns, I did not hold up my end of the bargain.

My last attempt was to try the laser. Thank God they performed a patch test because it left a white mark. Had I chosen the procedure, I would have no pigment left in my face at all. "Clown Face" is the layman's term. Maybe you can picture a certain performer I might have resembled?

Man, I cannot believe I just said that. Maybe the editor will take it out.

I conceded to the fact I was stuck with them.

> **Never occurred to me to simply love them as I loved my "flawed" eye and the two different colors.**

light bulb

If I loved those scars, maybe I would find a new strength in myself. I could talk about it and help other people. If I told people it did not bother me, just like the patch, I would believe it. Say it enough, until it became truth. Isn't that what I said the patch did? Why wasn't I doing it now? Nope, that was too simple,

Chapter Four

I still had more to learn.

tool time with tessie

I was developing a few poor patterns, huh? We all do it. Keep reading and working and you will learn to break yours as well.

Paint a self-portrait. I wonder what you will see.

You know what time it is. TOOL TIME! We now have added wood glue, a drill bit and a screwdriver.

Self empowerment

drill bit

wood glue

screwdriver

Which lesson do you want to screw into our life, George?

 **I AM PERFECT, JUST AS I AM!**

Say it with confidence and believe what you say.
Self image is an area I am constantly working on as well, but I am becoming stronger every day.

**Hey, you…smile!
Journal a little about your own "scars."**

Be Strong. Live.

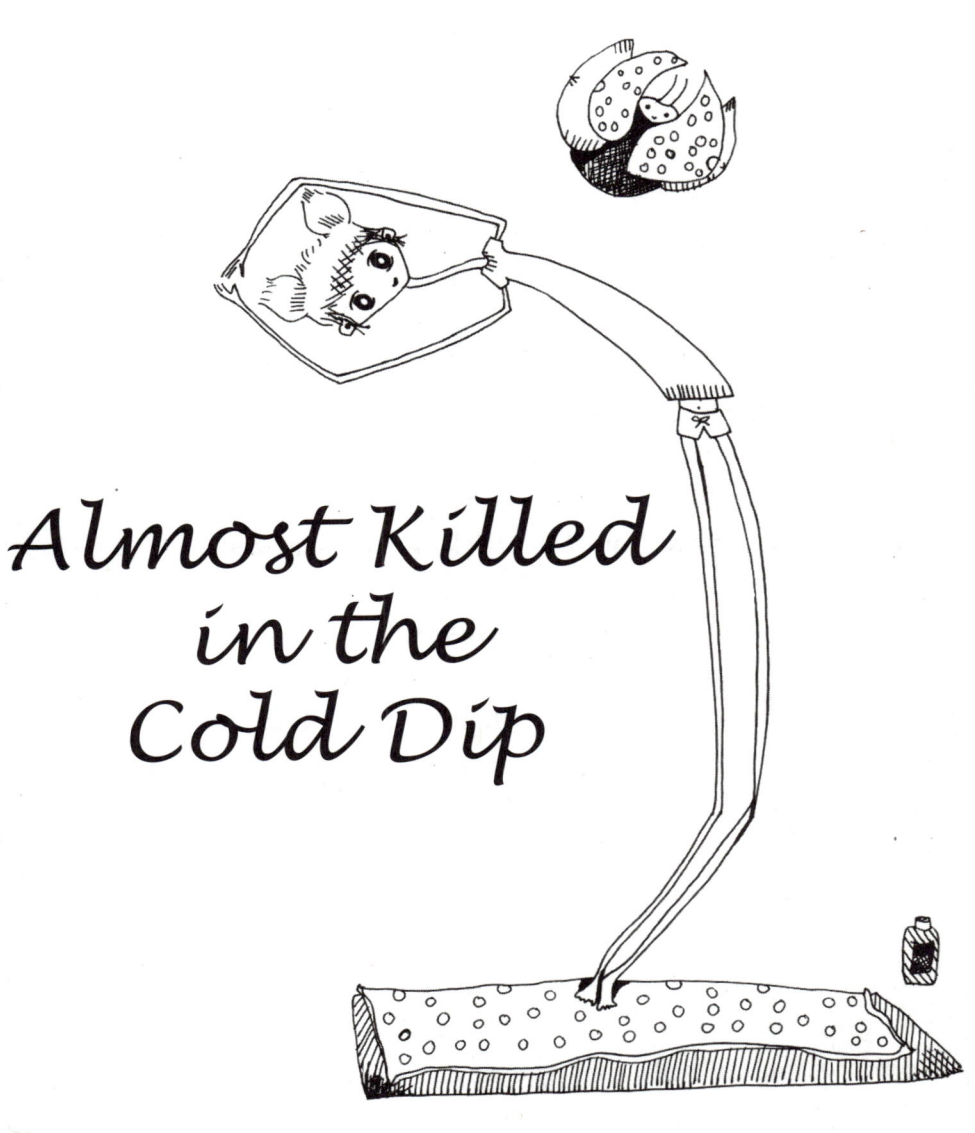

Almost Killed in the Cold Dip

What almost kills you makes you stronger, but only if you allow yourself to feel the pain it caused.

It is pouring rain and I am driving to work via the interstate. I am now 26 years old. I have a job I love, am good at, and I really had to tap dance to get it. We will get to that later. I am in the fast lane and my car begins to hydroplane. My SUV and I spiral into 360s all over the highway. I see headlights of other cars and it is a miracle no one hit me. To this day I still cannot imagine how that was possible. I ended up hitting the guardrail going about 50 miles per hour, head on. My truck was on the verge of flipping over the rail, when it suddenly just landed flat, like a miracle. BOOM. Everything was still.

No one stopped to check on me and thank God I was wearing my seatbelt. There was a moment when I thought I was going to die. I mean I really did think, *this is it*. My mind went blank but I had a vision of being blissfully happy with no regrets.

Now, a side note. I think this is also a success, being in that moment and having utter peace. Some people do not have one day in their life when they are happy, with no regrets. I had that moment in the face of death and it makes me smile to this day. Do you think erasing the fear of death is a success? Think about it.

Success!

I was not seriously injured. Because no one stopped to be my witness, Mr. Officer Not-So-Friendly gave me a ticket for careless driving and made me pay for the guardrail. Ah.

Chapter Five

My guardrail. I visit it often, now that I have paid for it and watched it be replaced. We are old friends, my guardrail and me. Okay. None of this is very relevant to the lesson the accident taught me. I simply think Mr. Officer Not-So-Friendly is an @$$. I wanted to scratch his eyes out when he calmly explained to me, although I slowed to 50 mph on an interstate due to the rain, I should have known to slow to 40 mph. Because, as everyone knows, you cannot hydroplane when traveling at a speed of only 40 mph. If I had done, as I so obviously knew to do, we would not be replacing his precious guardrail. Therefore, I am a careless driver. Did you know that bit of information?

Well, you do now, George. Next time it is raining and you are traveling at the rate of 70 mph, slow to 40 mph. Nope, 50 mph will not help you at all, and you will end up with a new friend named Guardrail.

"George, she scares me sometimes. Talking to guardrails? That is weird," you say with a funny look on your face.

I know. But loving that guardrail helped me let go of my anger. Ahh. Letting go. Easier said than done.

Okay, on to the lesson. I was not *seriously* injured, but I was injured. My neck was locked up, cocked to the side and I was in tremendous pain. I could not stand up straight and function like that, obviously. My chiropractor would not even touch it until I had a massage therapist unlock it a bit.

So, a friend gave me the number to a woman named Marie. Seriously, she is one of the best women I will ever know, now a close friend and soul sister of mine. She is a brilliant artist as well. Anyway, at the time, all I knew was she made house calls and I needed in- home care, so... done. Marie is the massage therapist of choice.

She came over and was completely different than any health care professional I had ever encountered. Any other time I had a physical ailment, I heard, "Now tell me what your problem is? Um-hm. Ok. Now, what were you doing when the pain started? Um-hm. Ok. Where is the pain exactly, and is it dull or sharp? Um-hm." Not Marie.

She asked me not to speak. She had me lie face up on the table she brought with her, and closed her eyes. She breathed audibly and placed her hands on my sternum. I was like ... ummmm ... crazy lady, hello! You can obviously see MY NECK is stuck to one side and I cannot stand up straight. I did not believe my sternum was out of place or weird looking.

She sensed my confusion and explained she performs Reiki, a form of energy work. She said she used her energy and the energy around us to heal my pain. We are, after all, energy, just a bunch of cells. Energy. I remembered this vaguely from a class or something. She instructed me to breathe with her and trust her. I thought she was nuts, but

Chapter Five

I am very open minded, so what the heck?

I followed her instructions as she worked on my chest and then seemed to follow her fingers to my ears, and flicked her hands off of my body. She asked me if I had been traumatized in any way or having nightmares. I said yes. She explained fear was a strong emotion and we store fear in our chest and upper body. Interesting. I had heard of emotions causing physical pain; I was listening more now.

I was injured, but the real problem was to actually release the fear from my body. If we did this, then the neck would "unstick." Worth a try. Sounded cool. Was she like a psychic? No, she said, she was an energy reader. I was to learn about that, trust me.

"This book just got weird," says George.

I know it did, but stay with me. You do not have to believe in it, but let me tell you what happened. Keep an open mind.

You guessed correctly; it worked! After twenty minutes of breathing and touching, I could move my neck. I was amazed, shocked really. I could

crowbar

Many of you need to pry open your closed mind. Also used to pry up rotted materials compromising our patterns also stand up straight. My body was still stiff and sore, but she said she could perform regular massage on me and fix the discomfort in no time. Wow. I loved her right then and there. She was incredibly kind, striking, loving and full of life. Her energy was contagious and I wanted to know her better, I had to. She had something to teach me and I knew it. I obviously went to her for subsequent massages.

One day she said to me, "Sarah, do you mind if I ask you a personal question?"

"Sure, why not?"

"I notice you have scars on your face and seem to suffer from cystic acne. Do you mind if I tell you that you have a digestive problem?" she asked.

"No. I have a hormonal problem. The doctors told me."

She disagreed with me and touched the front of my hip with her fingers. Pain shot through my hip while my face caught on fire.

"What are you doing to me? Hey, that hurts!" I cried.

She said she was hardly touching me at all. "That is your ileocecal valve. It controls the waste leaving your colon and is not functioning at ALL. You have a digestive problem.

Chapter Five

There are reflexes in your colon and this one is connected to your face. I bet you do not use the restroom three times a day, do you?"

"What?" First off, no one had ever talked to me about my colon! EEWWW, and speaking of number two, she was right. I did not go three times a day; I went about once a week!

I was to learn how very BAD that was. VERY BAD. You eat three times a day. You should have waste three times per day. If you do not, where is the waste? If the skin is the biggest elimination system in the body, wouldn't it HAVE to come out there?

The waste was coming out in my face! LIGHT BULBS! Now, that made sense to me. From here on out, when we have an "AH-HA" moment or a "wake-up call," we are going to receive a light bulb. Hold onto them. We will need them, trust me.

light bulb

She also told me my diet was HORRIBLE and was contributing to the entire problem. Dermatologists told me it was not my diet. Finding the truth to that lie has now changed my life. This is not a book to debate this ongoing battle with modern medicine. I will tackle that in a subsequent book, but you need to understand, this was all beginning to make a lot of sense to me. I was finding my passion, reason for being on this earth, message and purpose in life.

She instructed me to keep coming to her and trust. I did. I read everything I could get my hands on about the colon, the skin, and eating. I listened to CDs and watched videos.

My brain was becoming re-trained. We are alkaline, yet we dump acid in our body every day. Certain foods are acidic. We are a battery and will corrode if we become acidic. You hear it all the time. Acid reflux, Tums, antacids … more light bulbs. Those resources changed my entire pattern. I would change my diet COMPLETELY and the way I thought about the body.

This is not a book about how I want to help you change your diet, per se. I am now a wellness coach, I can reserve that for clients. I will touch on it in this book, we simply do not have time to delve into the inner workings of the body.

Marie worked with me for six months. I tested all my knowledge in my own body and began to connect the mind to the physical. She worked on my colon, my ileocecal valve and the cysts in my face. She weaned me off my medications and I never took another pill. She also gushed to me about hot yoga.

I said, "I can't do yoga! I am a Christian, not a Buddhist." She laughed. "You don't have to be a Buddhist to practice yoga, Sarah. It will help you find a deeper relationship with

Chapter Five

God as you know Him. Also, the poses have a medical purpose."

There are poses which will keep my ileocecal valve functioning, keep the cysts cleaned out and heal the lower spinal pain I also had. That particular pain was with me from age 11, the age I was diagnosed with osteochondrosis. In layman's terms, it is a curvature of the spine, similar to scoliosis. I was seeing a chiropractor for that. To make it all sound better, I would keep a tight body and become the weight I should be. Some people lost weight, and some gained.

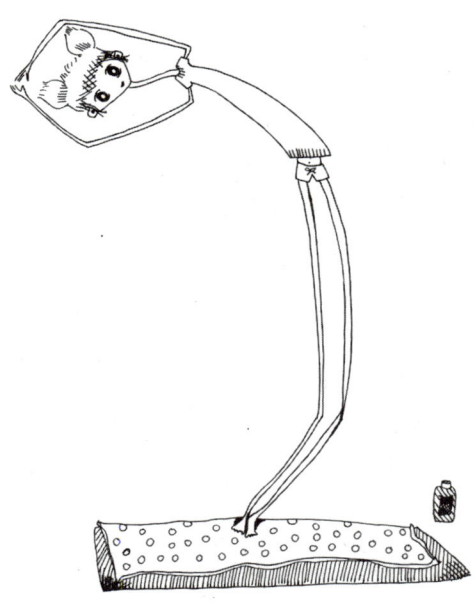

To sum up, she was telling me there was an exercise whichwould fix my acne by cleansing toxins, fix my colon so I would go to the bathroom three times per day, heal my back, keep me out of pain, balance my body to the weight it should be, and bring me closer to God. Oh, and she also said it would help me control my type A personality, have a little compassion for myself and not be overly critical. All of that from one 90-minute exercise class called yoga?
Sign me up!

"Um, yeah. ... George, this you have to see to believe!" I now gush.

The studio is having its opening day and I am one of the first people in town to try this type of yoga. I meet Anne, the owner. You would have to know her to understand how I feel about her. Just like Marie, she was wonderful, kind and compassionate, loving, striking and spiritual. We did not come from the same religious backgrounds but we became soul sisters despite this. Her energy? Beautiful.

She is the sort of person I say this to: "I feel honored you would even consider me a friend." Because I have to say, she has such a tremendous amount of insight that merely hearing her speak, makes you a better person. She has given me an enormous amount of light and I will be learning from her for years to come. She will be embarrassed and ask me to remove her from this book; simply the type of person she is. I am not going to listen to her.

Chapter Five

Her name is Anne. Call her. She will change your life.

I am now addicted to yoga. I have been called a Yoga's Witness. I tell everyone about it. I teach classes. It did do all of those things she promised, but oh, my dear lordy, it is hard. The room is 105 degrees. My heart is beating wildly the entire time. I sweat more than I ever have in my entire life. The 90 minutes seems like 90 years and many call it a TORTURE CHAMBER. They say this, because it is.

To heal my back, well, can you say *painful*? I never wanted to quit, though. She told me it was going to require work and would not be easy. I could revert back to taking medication if I wanted. That was easy, but I already told you it did not cure anything. I wanted a cure, not the easy fix. The *easy fix* was not helping.

I was willing to do the work. I needed to retrain my muscles to realign the spine and hold it there. The muscles wanted to keep pulling my spine back to where it had been for 26 years; that is what it knew. Muscle memory, they call it. It hurt to the point tears would stream down my face but I would not quit. I knew it was working, I had to stick with it.

See what I said? Muscle memory. Sometimes we will break old patterns, and they will revert back. You must continue making the choice until it becomes habit. Bear this in mind. There are hundreds of books out there on the subject of breaking habits. It is not always easy to build a new step, or pattern. I suppose you can now see we will be discussing this very subject as we move along. We will get there.

I want to share something with you. It may seem out of place in this story, but I promise it will connect you to the following truth and principle ... **Sometimes the things which are the hardest and most painful are what make us stronger.** My stories make this book relevant. Instead of going backward and finding a story to teach you this principle of allowing yourself to feel the pain, I am going to fast-forward to 2006. Scene: an upscale health resort in Tucson, Arizona. Not a shabby place to learn a lesson, eh?

Often you discover inspiration in the oddest of places. A friend of mine texted me and said he hoped I would find inspiration in the desert. I told him I would, if I just listened ... and was still ... and quieted my mind to hear.

I am in the ladies' locker room here at the resort. You have to understand, this locker room is nicer than my entire house! All the steam rooms, inhalation rooms, saunas, whirlpools, lockers, showers, nude sunbathing, mud and salt treatments, cucumber laid everywhere on ice for your eyes, cold towels for your face as you sit in the heat, ice, every kind of drink you could want (water, hot teas, lemonades,

Chapter Five

sports drinks), quiet rooms with blankets on couches for reading and meditating, robes, slippers, awesome service, etc. It is a true sanctuary.

No one wears clothes at all in here. We are all bare, naked and vulnerable. Because, let's face it, you cannot hide anything when you are naked. We all have flaws, all of us. There is something so liberating about being that vulnerable for all to see. No makeup. Did you read that? I was not wearing makeup. No clothes to hide flaws. I sit here and reflect, talk to women and hear their stories. I actually do not know why I even have a bathroom in my suite. I have not used it once since I have been here.

Anyway, there is a cold dip pool in the locker room, between two hot tubs. It is a plunge pool and measures 45 degrees. Does not sound too cold, does it? Nah. Well, let me tell you—— it is awful! I put my feet in because someone said it would "set" the paint on my pedicure. "Make sure you stay in for 30 seconds," she said. Easy enough. I only made it 15. It honestly felt as if thousands and thousands of tiny knives were attacking my feet from every angle and severing them from the ankle bones! I could not believe how horrible it was. Who was the sadistic freak who put his torture chamber in my sanctuary?!

light bulb

I hear of all the health benefits, if you submerge yourself, up to your chin, and return to the hot tub. You must stay in for one full minute. Sixty seconds. I heard it heals pain, gets the heart pumping and circulation moving, and flushes out toxins and cellulite.

I watched as women told me this, and then promptly chickened out after a mere 15 seconds, as I did. 15 seconds is the moment knives begin attacking you. Seriously. They just start attacking! So trust me, I neither blamed them for it, nor did I judge them for failing. I mean, it hurts! There were the others, the ones who lied to themselves. They told themselves if they jumped in and jumped out, they actually accomplished something. Those were the ones I did not understand. Why lie to yourself? You knew you did not do anything worthwhile and so did all the ones watching.

Then today, a woman walked out of the hot tub we were sharing——104 degrees——naked——walked over to the sadistic, Antarctic waters of the cold dip, and slowly submerged herself up to her chin. She remained there, calmly, for the full minute. Wow. WOW! She patiently watched the clock and came back to the hot tub. She repeated this process 3 times and it took about 20 minutes to complete the cycle. Hot, cold, hot, cold, hot, cold … I was amazed!

I asked her why the heck she put her body through something so horrible? Through something I knew I could

Chapter Five

not stomach?

Her reply? Pain. Arthritis. It was really helping her. She said those 20 minutes of hell give her days of relief, relief she has not been able to find anywhere. She said it was difficult at first, but she desperately needed it and willed herself to do it.

You know, sometimes the hardest, most painful things are what help us most. What a simple truth, right? But why do we forget it when the pain actually begins to take hold? Why do we only "stay in" for about 15 seconds, when staying in for a full minute seems impossible? It is not that simple, is it?

drill bit

Motivation
What does it take to motivate you to change?

To achieve true healing, we must look at ourselves, feel the pain, listen and change. It is much easier to "jump out," gloss over it, self-medicate and "move on." You tell yourself because you merely went in, you accomplished something. What does not kill you will make you stronger, right? Or does it? Does it make you stronger simply because it did not kill you, or do you gain strength from looking at what almost killed you and actually feel the pain it caused? Then do the work to relieve the pain, and grow stronger from *that*? That is what I discovered.

So, I thought, you know, I am going to do this! I have deep toxins in here which need to be released and I could use the flush. Makes sense, right? If she can, I can. So, I did and it was horrible. Oh my gawd, it was awful. I could not even breathe. It felt as if my lungs were caving in and collapsing. It was tremendously difficult to stay in and the knives came back. All the way from my chin to my toenails—daggers.

She told me to breathe and relax my muscles. It was outrageously hard to relax, but I did and watched the clock——longest minute of my life! I would rather relive my labor pains than this, but I was determined. I did it ... 3 times and every time became easier, much easier. I relaxed and felt the pain, knowing the benefit was just a minute away.

WOW! All tension and stress were erased. My pain in the lower back? Gone. I even received a workout. My heart rate was up for 20 minutes straight. I could not believe how tired I had become. I DID IT! **It was such a rush, a huge sense of accomplishment.** It's strange that I felt I accomplished a great feat from sitting in a cold pool, but I did.

Sweat

Hard work is essential to break patterns

I must be honest and admit, I am so relieved that is not my therapy needed for any serious pain. I do not know how she

Chapter Five

does it, but I see it really works. I did it with her every day I saw her——three days of it——and we became friends.

Back to 2001. Do you see the spiritual truth there? I was going through a divorce at the time I found that inspiration. We will get to that, but even back in 2001, I saw that truth. Not only was I healing my physical body through feeling all of the pain and doing the work, I was healing my spirit as well. Yoga was changing me—— or I should say—— *I* was changing me.

PATTERN CHANGE time.

Also, yoga does not teach competition as the gym does. I was being compared to those women in the gym or the locker room. Most gyms breed this unhealthy mentality: comparing and wanting what someone else has, wanting his/her body. It feeds society's lies. Yoga did not teach me that. It taught me things my parents taught me, what the Bible taught me.

> I was me, fearfully and wonderfully made.
>
> I was like no one in the room and that was a good thing.
>
> Love myself so I can love my neighbor.
>
> Stop and smell the roses.
>
> Still your mind to hear the lesson you are to receive.
>
> If you fall, pick yourself back up.
>
> You are a success.
>
> Honor yourself and others.

Chapter Five

All of those lessons I had learned my entire life were being taught to me in an exercise class. Amazing.

It taught me I was not too skinny. I was maintaining the healthy body I was supposed to have, *my* body. I do not even own a scale anymore. I love my skinny body now and desire to put healthy foods into it. My back straightened out and I am an inch taller. That curve shortened my spine, think about it. My cysts cleared up, the medications disappeared. I had compassion for myself in class and was taught to push myself only when necessary. No more crying during a potato sack race or after getting an *F*. No more living in torment over failures.

Each day was a new day, and my practice would be different every day. I was to look at *me* in the mirror and see myself through my eyes only. I am discouraged from looking around the room. I barely wear clothes, all "flaws" are visible and I am forced to look at them. I am crying as I write to you, because I truly came to love myself through all of this. If you ever have come to this point—loving something about yourself you once hated—you know my tears.

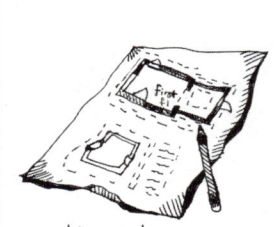

blueprint

My life is a blueprint to build something very important. I encourage you to make changes and create a unique blueprint

I will build a wellness center to help others find their path because of my "too skinny" of a body, because of my scars, because I allowed myself to feel the pain and grow from it ... and because I broke this negative pattern and turned it into a positive one. We will get to that.

I took my power back. My parents are proud of me again and guess what? I practice with no makeup and I go out in public without it often. Go ahead, ask me about my "imperfection," I will tell you. I do not have a ladybug stuck to my face this time. The patch was temporary. I have scars now and they are permanent, as are the ones on my heart. We will address them soon.

Go ahead, ask me. I want to tell you how these scars make me strong. Notice how I came full circle.

The same is true with this as it is with my eye. If a surgeon came up to me and told me he could make my face perfect, I would tell him *no*. No, thank you. I love my face just as it is. **My scars tell a story and are a reminder of who I have become.** I am happy just as I am. I am fearfully and wonderfully made. The word "imperfection" is now an asset.

I am 33 years old, I have scars stuck to my face and you don't.

I am really cool.

Chapter Five

We are going to come back to all of this later. I still have more patterns needing to be changed, so we must go back a little, find them and see if we can do some repair. Okay? I promise we will come back, because this is my purpose for being here——coaching others with their health, *in whole*, mind, body and spirit. It makes me fulfilled to do so.

So, let us connect to our lesson here, these simple—or not so simple—truths:

The things which are the hardest and most painful are what we really need in order to grow.

Doing the work benefits us much more in the long run.

There truly is not an easy way out.

What does not kill us, makes us stronger … but in my current, humble observation, ONLY if you choose NOT to ignore what almost killed you.

tool time with tessie

Are you beginning to see the light? I know I am. Knowing why you were put here on this earth is a gift. Working hard has become second nature to me and I hope the same happens for you. Time for *you* to do a little work.

Find a painful experience in your life and turn it into a positive. You never know what you might discover.

Let's place our tools into the box and add a little sweat while we do it, shall we? Light bulbs, crowbar, a drill bit, and a blueprint to get you started.

I personally want to screw in the following to my new pattern:

 **MY "SCARS" TELL A BEAUTIFUL STORY!**

I speak it aloud every day and go on my merry way. It may seem corny, but I love myself, just as I am. Do you?

**If you cannot honestly say yes, write,
but be prepared to feel a little pain as you grow.**

Be Aware.
Feel.

Stop and Watch the Lilies

Quiet your mind.
If you do not, you will miss life's biggest lessons.

"George, I think she means *stop and smell the roses*," you say.

I know. That is what most people say, but by now you should know my mother never really taught us in the manner other moms did. She was not better than anyone else, she simply had alternative methods of doing things. She liked being different. Remember? She taught me that and it is time to really talk about her. I am not sure how many pages it will take, we will just have to see.

I know we pretty much solved a big problem in my life about the scars and purpose, right? Well, we need to back up a bit and talk about where much of my strength came from and how having healthy patterns in place, aid in breaking poor ones. I still have more to break. Don't you wish it was just one? Me too. Okay, so back we go.

> **DO NOT ALLOW THE LACK OF MONEY TO BE YOUR EXCUSE FOR NOT DOING WHAT YOU WERE DESIGNED TO DO!**

My mom. She is one of a kind to be sure. She was the epitome of our statement, "What others think of me is none of my business." She lived and breathed it. We would become embarrassed by the old cars or old furniture. She never did. I am sure she wanted better, who doesn't? She was not perfect but I never saw my mother act ashamed of

Chapter Six

anything. Well, not unless we shamed her with our behavior, which I know we did. You know what I mean.

She was proud and, man, was she ever creative. She was the type of person to say, "Glen (that is my dad), stop the car! Someone threw away that old bookcase. We have to get it." My dad would roll his eyes, and we would stop the car as she jumped out. He knew there was no sense in arguing with her. It would be strapped onto the car somehow and end up as a piece of furniture in our house. She could do things to that bookcase and one would never know it had been in the trash. She was creative. It is a tool. Defining her own lines, remember?

She did not like to tell us *no*. I remember wanting desperately to join a swim team. Who knows? Maybe I was to be a swimmer in the Olympics. Sarah, the Breast Stroking Gold Medalist.

"Here we go again, George, with the star," you say as you roll your eyes.

I am kidding. Relax. The swim team I wanted to join was a successful one, second in our division. Meets were held at the best, most private country clubs in town. We would rotate "home" pools and, when the season ended with the big meet——the championships. It was set up similar to the real Olympics with heats and finals.

There were medals and ribbons for the winners. It was a big deal to us kids and I wanted to be on that team.

I actually was a decent breaststroker. My mom wanted me to live up to my potential and did not want to tell me *no*. She knew it would be a healthy environment to keep setting all these healthy patterns I keep talking to you about. She believed the swim team would provide the following principles:

Give me more tools for my toolbox.
Give opportunities to fail and succeed.
Small successes were recognized.
I could be a winner without putting someone else down
Believe in myself.
Love myself and my teammates.
Be compassionate with myself when I did not win.
Finish and do my best.

My parents could prove to me they did love me and were proud of me, even when I did not come home with the first-place medal. They had been trying to hand off this tool to me since the sack race.

So, what to do for money? She could not go to "Barely New" for this one. Well, my mother did not care what anyone thought of her, right? She marched herself into a local pool company, Wellman Pools.

Chapter Six

"Hi. My name is Peggy Friese. This is my daughter Sarah. She is a great breaststroker and she wants to join the swim team. She needs a sponsor. Now, for only $20 per month, she will let you sponsor her. She will wear one of your Wellman Pools T-shirts to every swim meet in this town. Did I mention the swim meets are held at the most wealthy country clubs in town? Oh yes, they are. I will tell people you are her sponsor and I bet someone will want you to build their next pool, or at the very least, allow you to service the one they already have. What a cheap way for you to advertise, don't you think?"

Um, yeah. *That* is my mom.

She did not lower herself or make me feel ashamed we had no money. Now, I will let you in on the secret I have been keeping. I DID NOT KNOW WE DID NOT HAVE MONEY! She did not tell me. She definitely broke some patterns of her own to believe this way about having little money. She always saw the positive in just about everything. It can get annoying at times because she does it so often. It is only annoying because you know *you* cannot be as positive as she is. I am trying, though. Don't imagine I will ever catch up to her.

So, I wore this T-shirt to every swim meet. I remember the shirt had a devil on it, a Wellman mascot or something. My mom did not like me wearing a devil, and neither did God, she said. So she took a patch and covered it up——another patch. The one she chose was a Number One Blue Ribbon. I mean, here I was with this shirt with a ribbon proclaiming I was number one already.

I was actually really cool. I was the only kid with a sponsor. Different. Again, different was good. The other mothers wanted to know about my sponsor and it gave her the opportunity to talk about the pools.

Again, that attribute, talking about an imperfection——not having money——gave her an opportunity to turn it into a strength. Only, she did not need to mention the fact we had little money. I am sure people could tell by our cars or whatever else people use to judge these things. She never acted ashamed, though. The other mothers loved her and admired her, they listened to her. She had a message. She *always* had a message. To this day, we will never know how many of those families switched over their pool service to Wellman, or how many bought pools down the road. I like to imagine everyone did.

It came time for the championship meet, and now the entire team needed money. Who do you think the other mothers turned to? You guessed it, my mom. She marched herself into Dr. Pepper this time and BAM, we had a team sponsor. I remember wearing Dr. Pepper T-shirts, drinking Dr. Pepper, saying "I'm a Pepper" and not know why I was

Chapter Six

saying it. We have zillions of pictures with those shirts on. I am sitting there with the whole team, smiling.

I won a lot of ribbons, trophies and medals. I was the most improved swimmer the very first year. Right off the bat I won that special award. I won first place ribbons most of the time and was proud, but I even saved the heat winner ribbons because they made me feel proud, too. My parents and the swimming finally helped me understand first was not the only success. They were proud when I simply finished the race. I knew that, and I put the tool in my toolbox. Still wanted to be first, though. He-he.

I was successful for years. To this day I have a scrapbook filled with almost every ribbon. Our coach even used me as an example to show the other swimmers the perfect breaststroke. I was a natural at it, for some reason and was proud.

drill bit

Perseverance
We are not quitters

This was all a success and my mom helped make it one. She did not say *no*, once again. The lack of money did not file away in her head as a negative thought; she chose not to believe it. She simply did not buy into that way of thinking and I am the better for it. She set a pattern and made those choices. That creativity tool went into my toolbox. I do not ever have to swim another day or participate in the Olympics, to be a great swimmer. I was great because of all I took with me, lessons that may have been missed if mom was not so incredibly creative.

"You love her, don't you, George? It's okay. I do too."

ONLY YOU CAN CHANGE YOUR PATTERNS

Now let's talk about the patterns my mom had to break to teach me thus far. We can also discuss the ones she chose to keep. You need a little insight into some of her childhood to accomplish this. I am not going into full detail because my mom does not talk to just anyone about the things she lived through. This is her choice and I respect it.

What I can tell you is her mother never told her she loved her until my mom was in her fifties, not one day until then. Wow, I cannot imagine this. Maybe you can. Maybe your mom did the same thing to you, and you can now relate to my mother. Maybe she still has not told you. Maybe you will relate to my mom more than you do me. Great. I am sure by the time you read this entire book, you will want to meet her long before you ever want to meet me. Trust me, this is a wise choice.

She was not told she could do everything and anything. She

Chapter Six

walked across the tracks to a better school for a better education, and was ashamed of where she lived. She lived in the boxcar of a train. She was ashamed of her clothes and she worked hard to buy herself new ones. As I understand it, none of her friends knew she was this poor; she hid it well. She will tell you her mom always made sure they had what they needed, when they needed it. My grandmother was a creative woman, a very hard worker.

Now, at the end of this chapter, I want to discuss the patterns in these two paragraphs, healthy and unhealthy. A few were broken and some not. Can you see them? I can, so clearly. But for a minute, let's get back to her being my mom, and what she did for me.

> **A TRUE LEADER HAS FOLLOWERS.**
> **A *GREAT* LEADER IS BEGGED BY THEM TO LEAD**

So, my mom became the Professional Volunteer Mom. She was great at everything, especially organizing. She was a leader and the other mothers followed. In fact, they begged her to lead. They allowed Alison and me to join whichever activity we were interested in for free, if my mom agreed to lead the entire team. Wow. Now, that is a leader—when others are begging you to lead. I paid attention.

Do you think that is a success? I certainly do. So many people never have one day in their life when they are

Success!

viewed as a leader. One must have followers to be considered a leader. My mom had them, boy, did she.

Because of this trait of hers, we did just about anything we ever wanted to do. We were on the golf team, tennis team, had cello and violin lessons, etc. Sometimes my poor sister had to join the teams I did, simply because my mom agreed to be the lead volunteer. If my mom did this for me, well, who would watch poor Alison? She had no choice but to come along. Sorry, Alison, right here and now, sorry about the golf. She hated it.

drill bit

Leadership
Lead with a purpose and they will follow

My mom was the queen of tap dancing and she did not even know it. Do you see where I saw that pattern? I mean, she did not play any of these sports, except tennis. She did not act, play music, none of it. Nevertheless, she led everyone into the competitions of a sport of which she knew nothing and we usually won. Talk about tap dancing. Talk about success. Talk about using her tools and she showed me how to use them. I continued to pay attention and admired her.

Chapter Six

Now, she did love tennis. She was asked to be the head volunteer of a tennis championship in Amelia Island, Florida, about 45 minutes from where we lived. The tournament is a very big deal. It is a ladies tournament and all the widely recognized stars played in it. There was also the secondary tournament, which was there for a while, and it attracted the male stars. We had the opportunity to become ball kids. She was so cool. She did not mind we had to miss these two weeks of school just to fetch the players' balls. She believed it was important for us to be balanced and learn through *life* and not just our schooling.

Man, every kid in school was jealous. We would return to class and I promise you, we had pictures of us with Andre Agassi, Stefan Edberg, Ivan Lendl, Martina Navratilova, Gabriela Sabatini, Steffi Graf—and Jimmy Connors even puked in my towel. I saved it forever.

"Gross. George, she saved his puke," you wince.

Yes, I did. We saved many sweaty towels. It made us feel as if Andre Agassi lived in our closet. When it began to smell as if he lived there, my mom forced us to throw them out. Aw, Mom!

When we were not working, she would find us box seats to sit in and watch them play. Here we were, Alison and I, poorer than dirt, and we were in box seats at a big tournament, taking pictures with all of these famous athletes. We were in heaven.

We learned to serve other people this way. We were expected to work hard, no goofing off. We served those players with respect and work ethic was instilled in us at an early age. We were responsible to show up where we were assigned, on time. No one was watching over us and babying us. If you could not manage your own time, don't be a ball kid. We could not be late, or we would never be picked to ball kid at the centre court. Anyone who watches tennis, knows all the stars play at the centre court. We learned to work together as a team. We were learning so many of the lessons our parents were already teaching us.

It even helped me with depth perception with my eye. Seriously. I had to throw the ball in just one bounce to the player, I promise. Two bounces and some players made you do it again. One girl peed her pants, literally, because a player made her do it ten times. I had difficulties at first, but I got the hang of it. Huh. I had never really connected that lesson until now, not until I just wrote it. Thank you, mean tennis star, you helped me with my bum eye. Thank you. My mom thought it was important we saw these lessons in real life, and she found this way to teach us. Now do you see why she kept us out of school?

Chapter Six

IF YOU DO NOT GIVE WHEN YOU DO NOT HAVE, YOU WILL NOT GIVE WHEN YOU DO

My mother was also very giving. I mean, boy did she give. The main reason we were poor is my dad had a heart to be a missionary. We were to eventually pack up and move to Mexico. That is his passion in life, and we will get to him. He knew his purpose, his reason for being here. He has a message. My mom had to sacrifice for it and I see that now. We will get back to that thought, sacrifice, I promise.

Anyway, she said God says you should give. He will give back to you tenfold, if you do. We were able to see this lesson in action, because in a way, God really did pay our salary.

My dad was pacing the floor, stressed out, before we were to leave for Mexico. "Peggy, how could you give away our last bit of money? Are you crazy? What will we do? I mean, that was pretty much all of it."

"Now, Glen. Mrs. So-and-so needed a new washer and dryer. I heard God telling me I should give her the money. He did tell me that, clearly. He said it would be a lesson to us all and He would give us back tenfold. I mean, do you not have any faith?" she retorted.

Well, what could he say to that? I mean, *he* was the missionary, not she. *He* was the one preaching about faith, not she. *He* was saying God talks to us and we had better listen when He does, not she. Mom was merely doing what she was taught as I did with my Tessie story. Remember? This is another pattern I observed. What could he say?

I am not exaggerating this time. The very next day, we had a check in our PO Box for exactly ten times the amount she gave away. We will never know who sent it because it was a cashier's check. She behaved as if she knew it would happen; she was not surprised. She believed. It was always like that. I have a million stories like this, enough to fill a book. Dad will even tell you it was Mom who taught us about giving. She was generous, even when we had nothing.

Giving cheerfully
We give with a smile

So, I ask you and George, is someone like, let's say, Oprah more successful than my mom? I say *no* and I mean it. Is my mom more successful than Oprah? Again I say *no*.

I can clearly see Oprah has taken her talents, message and purpose, seeds if you will, and has sown them in a field

Chapter Six

which would reap fame. She has a message to speak to a large amount of people and she can reach them in greater numbers by doing exactly what she does.

My mother took those same seeds, but she planted them in soil which would harvest something very different, family. Notice, Oprah does not have children and is not married. My mom does not have a television show, yet both of them planted a school in a foreign country and it does not make a difference whose was larger.

The point is, they broke unhealthy patterns and changed them, kept the good ones and reaped a harvest which is plentiful. They are **both** successful, equally. They found their message and spoke it and honestly, I do not know many people who do not admire my mother. I bet you are becoming a huge fan, just by reading this book. I need you to believe what I am saying because what I just said in this paragraph, applies to you.

Success!

You can be as successful as an "Oprah." YOU.

APPRECIATE ANOTHER'S SACRIFICE

All of this brings me to talk about sacrifice. Do you not think I sit back and read what I have written and regret every time I was not kind to my mom? Hey, I was a teenager raised in a world of materialism just as any other youth. I hobnobbed with the rich. I was not sheltered; I was popular. I did not appreciate her sacrifice. What teenager does, really? I was not horribly ungrateful, but trust me, there are things I wish I had never done or said.

light bulb

My mom was injured while playing tennis. She hurt her knee, required surgery, and we could not afford the after therapy she needed to heal. She found a way to invent her own type of therapy. I felt horrible I did not assist her. She was in pain and needed my help, but I was a teenager and I did not think about those things. I thought about me and boys and school—teenage stuff. I wish I could go back, and help get her things so she did not need to walk downstairs. I wish I would have kept some of my passionate rants to a minimum and not wear her out or provoke her to napping. I wish so many things.

I have made a choice to change.

Chapter Six

When she simply cannot take it anymore or life gets rough, trust me, I am the first one there. I live the closest to her and maybe God allowed this on purpose. In this case, if I would have changed the pattern and then had no opportunity to put it into action **be**cause another sibling lived closer, I would not receive the blessing.

Mom, siblings, I am glad I am the one who lives **the** closest. I do not mind when I m**us**t step in. I really do not. I love the fact when Mom needs something or has a weak day—and she has them, she is like all of us—I love it she calls me first. Maybe I can make it all up to her.

drill bit

Sacrifice
We are not selfish

You remember the joke I made earlier, about the nursing home, it was just that——a joke.

I would do anything for her.

> **DO NOT MISTAKE SOMEONE ELSE'S PURPOSE FOR YOUR OWN AND VICE VERSA**

I want to stop the story right here for a bit.
Maybe you are sitting there mumbling to yourself, "Her mom is really great, George, but I don't think I could ever be like that."

I am glad you said that. What are you supposed to be like?

Circular Saw

Use your creativity and shape your patterns

When other mothers complained they could not afford to stay home with their children, my mom always replied with the following: "I can't afford *not* to stay home with mine." That was her message and I love her for it. She used her tools. Saying you could not afford to stay home was buying into something negative. Because if staying home was your purpose, and you allowed the lack of money to prevent you, well then, you were not using your tools, were you?

We were poorer than the women who complained, but my mom used her power drill and she decided being poor

Chapter Six

allowed her to use her creativity tool, one she loved to pull out. It was a fun tool: A circular saw. She has obviously spoken her message well by living it. *It is not necessary to have 'money' to stay home.*

Do I believe you or I need to stay home with our children? Good question. The answer is: If that is your purpose.

I hear of so many women staying home because their mothers did or the church taught them to, or because their husbands told them they must. I know women who want careers. But why do they want them? What is their message? Be sure when you are making these types of choices, you are staying true to your purpose. I know many women who work outside the home and I applaud them. They are successful and have found their purpose.

So, what is your message, your purpose? My mom knew hers and that is why I am proud of her. She was passionate about it and she lived it and breathed it. She embodied it and that is why she is successful. As for me, I do both; I work and stay home. I have found my purpose and message, though.

The debate I hear so often goes something like this: "I don't really want to have children."

"Oh, Betty, how can you say that? You *should* have children. Why don't you start right now?"

People. People. People. Leave Betty alone. Maybe she has not heard the "call" to have children. Maybe she never will.

Allow these people to listen to God. Give them time and space. God will tell them what their purpose is concerning children——in *their* time. Maybe He has already told them. Leave them alone. Hey, I have a son, and up until about a month ago, I swore I would never do it again, never. People looked at me as if I were Satan. But I have done some growing and listening, and in the right circumstance I would have another child. I said, *in the right circumstance.*

Maybe you will discover you never want children. Great. I have many friends who have found that same answer. As long as you know your purpose, I applaud you, but do not become annoyed with me for changing my mind.

Let's stay busy looking at our own lives and leave others to look at theirs. Embrace the differences. Different is good, remember? Deal? Now, let's get back to my amazing mother.

Chapter Six

BEING STILL IS HARDER THAN YOU MIGHT IMAGINE, BUT, OH, THE BENEFITS!

My mother and I were afforded the special opportunity to spend quiet time together in Mexico as my dad and sister were back in the States. There was not much to do and I was bored one night. My mom was never bored. That in itself amazes me——to never become bored. Another success. Some people never have one day in their life when they can find peace and happiness in just doing nothing. My mom is the queen of it and we were never allowed to say, "There's nothing to do."

Success!

She asked me to come outside. She was sitting there in the moonlight, staring at the lilies. They were blooming and I do not mean they were about to, or were in season. I mean they were blooming—popping open before our very eyes. I had never seen that before. I mean, you can see this when tape is sped up to cause it to bloom at a faster rate, but this was happening in our own backyard. We ran inside, made some tea, brought our dinner out there and watched the lilies bloom, one by one. The white petals would pop open and we stared in awe and wonder. Our yard was full of them and it was beautiful, one of the most beautiful sights I have ever seen.

We did this, night after night…watching the lilies, talking, laughing about the funny stories I am writing now, and the new ones we were experiencing in Mexico. We laughed when we heard the ice-man pass by our gate. He is just this guy, on a cart drawn by a donkey, with a big ole block of ice. He would yell as they trotted down the street and people run out, grab their ice and run back in.

The trash man followed suit. "BASURA," he would yell. Dump your trash on his cart, and he moves on. Soccer matches were always going and we would randomly hear GOAL over a loudspeaker. The turkey next door was gobbling. I am sure our rat—I named him Henry the Rat—scurried by. Mom even taught us to think of that rat in a positive way.

Actually it was a mouse, but I told you I have a tendency to exaggerate a bit.

All the goings on, interrupted our silence and we began to laugh. Here we were in this dirty, dirty place, with limited peace and quiet. I mean, everyone stared at us. We were always on display; we were very different. Again? Different. Yup, and we loved it. But we *did* find utter peace during those nights and I learned to be still. She said the Bible said, "Be still and know that I am God." Well, God, I think watching your creation bloom before my very eyes, was definitely getting to know You better.

Chapter Six

I like this lesson, because she was teaching me to meditate, be silent and hear. Yoga teaches this. People are constantly striving to master this very lesson. If one does, then one is enlightened, I am told. My mom simply did it. That is how she is. If God said it, well then she took it in faith, as a child. No questioning. He said be still, okay, I am still. This is a huge success. I would love to be more like she is. I have to practice yoga about four times a week to achieve it.

You know what? Had she not taught me to meditate, this book would not exist.

We all have stories, all of us. I am sure you have more than I ever will. Notice, many women sat by the cold dip and watched that woman go in, and thought nothing of it. I have now learned to quiet my mind and hear the lessons going on around me. Life really does teach us but we must take the time to hear.

I want to point out something I have come to understand. For me, prayer is the time I take to speak to God and express myself, wishes and passions. I often do this while "on the go." **Meditation is the part of my day when I physically stop and hear.** I welcome God to speak *to* me. I allow life around me to speak and allow a moment to hear and actually *listen*. If you took a moment to read David's Psalms, you would notice how  often he mentions his own personal meditation. Go to your dictionary and look up the word *selah*. You might have a different attitude towards yoga if you do.

I know many of you confuse meditation with prayer or are afraid of one or the other. I personally believe both are essential to my spiritual life and daily routine. I highly

Chapter Six

recommend you try it if you have not. It cannot hurt to try. I challenge those of you whom exclusively meditate, to pray. Take your crow bar and open your spirit to a new experience. Indulge me as I tell you **what meditation has done for me and my son.**

I drive Caleb to preschool almost every day now. We pass over the train tracks. Did I ever tell you how much my son loves trains? Well, he does. The look he gets on his face when he sees one, brings tears to my eyes. I see me in his face. His eyes are very big, like mine, and they become even bigger when he hears the whistle. He jumps up and down and is overexcited and passionate. Did I ever tell you I take a lot of naps?

Anyway, if we see a train stopped to the side, this indicates another train is approaching from the opposite direction. They are making a pass and the train we see is waiting. We never know how long it will be before the next one comes; it could be one minute, it could be thirty. But you know what, who cares? I pull out my "stop and watch

Lunch Break
Take it from my wonderful MOM, naps are great. Take a break. Re-charge your soul

the lilies" lunch break and pull over. I do not care if he is late to preschool. We wait and are quiet. I make a mental note to turn off my phone and watch him, and observe his face as it blooms. The train finally roars down the tracks.

"Woo-woo," he says. I do it too. I let him sit up front, stick his head out the sunroof and wave. The engineer always waves back. He knows Caleb and me by now, the little family who waits. We enjoy peace in that moment of noise when the train rumbles by. We laugh. We connect, then go about our day.

Do you see the lesson in that? Up until I had a child, I hated the train. But did I really hate the train? No, I hated the fact it made me slow down. My son just taught me that precious light bulb lesson. He gave me the "be still" lunch break.

Watch your children, they will teach you. Trust me, they are smarter than we are. They have not learned to stop questioning *why*. We will get to that… *why*—an important word, by George!

I want to add one thing. My mother's napping also taught us to take a break. While you are reading this, you might feel the need to stop for two reasons: To rest OR to be still and simply hear. I encourage you to do both. It has taken six years but I am learning to meditate and remain unaffected in even the noisiest of circumstances. Every experience is a new lesson in my growth. I LOVE IT!

Chapter Six

**IT CAN TAKE SEVERAL GENERATIONS TO BREAK ONE POOR PATTERN,
BUT ONLY *ONE* TO INSTILL A NEW, HEALTHY ONE**

I promised we would return to those paragraphs about my mom's patterns. Do you want to read them again? Here, why don't we list the poor patterns she changed.

1. *Her* mother did not tell her she loved her, until my mom was in her fifties.

PATTERN BREAK: She first needed to love herself——a very difficult feat to accomplish——then make a choice to say, "I love you," to me. I was told from the day I entered this world I was loved. *Notice something else.* <u>Her</u> *mom also broke this pattern. Took her a while, but she broke it and that was a success. Way to go, Grandma!*

Success!

2. *Her* mom never told her she could be anything she wanted to be and did not build her up.

PATTERN BREAK: She first had to believe she could, then make a choice to teach me. I am Tessie, the tap dancing orphan. Need I say more?

3. She was ashamed of where she lived and of her clothes.

PATTERN BREAK: I already told you quite clearly, my mom was not ashamed as she grew. She began to hold her head high and taught us by example.

Now let us look at the healthy patterns she chose to keep.

1. She knew she was poor but she did not let it get her down. She made the choice to attend a better school and work to purchase better clothes.

I have shown you the many ways she instilled in us to make choices, to better ourselves and just go do it.

2. Her mother was creative.

Um. Yeah. We have that one covered. Wellman Pools, patch, tap shoes, *Oliver!*, etc. My mother's creativity could be a whole other book and I am now very creative and resourceful. Thank you, Grandma.

3. Had what she needed when she needed it, because her mother was a hard worker.

My parents both embodied this principle. Boy, did they and now I do as well. Faith is a huge part of my life.

Chapter Six

She also created a new pattern by showing us to be thankful for what we had, essential tool for our toolbox. She made the choice to teach us to give as we discussed, even when we did not have anything to give.

My Grandma. She was an interesting lady. She broke all the patterns she could in her sixties and seventies and finally did tell my mom she loved her. She and her eight children became very close. She found God in her life. My mother became an example to her. It was not too late. She traveled the world, making friends along the way. She attended college and was loved by many people. Never did make a lot of money, but she was happy. She discovered joy.

Thankfulness
We are grateful for what we have been given

She died last year and my mother ached. But you know, they had a chance to establish a loving relationship and I witnessed my mom let go of old hurts, ones she did not think she was capable of letting go. I am glad they had that precious time.

Her funeral was uplifting and everyone who attended smiled. She watched it, I am sure, with pride.

> **IT IS NEVER TOO LATE TO SAY THANK YOU. TRUST ME, OTHERS NEED TO HEAR IT**

I want to end this chapter by using one of our tools, being thankful. I remember reading one of our presidents decided to cure the Monday blues by being thankful. He said if he wrote five thank-you notes to five people, well then, he just felt better. Being thankful made the trivial problems become just that, trivial. Great way to start a week, don't you think? He did this every Monday. I began doing it a while back and I challenge you to do the same. It actually works. It simply makes your entire day brighter and, therefore, your week brighter. As I am writing, I realize it is Monday. I promise and cross my heart, it is Monday.
So here goes.

Chapter Six

Mom,

Thank you. I know I told you this when I was 18, but I am telling you again. Thank you. I was very ungrateful to complain about doing the laundry when I was a teenager. Now I see, after living in Mexico, washing clothes out by hand is not fun! The washing machine back in the States was a blessing, just like you tried to teach me. I wasn't grateful and thankful for so many of the little things. I could have continued to be a spoiled, materialistic teenager, but Mexico saved me from that. I see that now.

Thank you for being an example. You always taught us to be thankful, to love others and give, to be still and hear God's voice...to hear the voice within us... in others...to love ourselves and to avoid buying into what others thought of us. You taught us we could do anything, be anything... how to serve others. Not only did you teach it, you lived it. I learned all of these things by watching you.

I am not perfect but I hope you are proud of what you did, where you sowed your seeds. Because, looking back, you could have done anything with all of these talents and gifts you possess. You could have sowed those seeds of talent in different soil and become famous, or what the world calls a star. But you chose to sow those talent seeds in the soil of me, of us, of family. That was your message and you reaped the harvest. I want to be something you are proud to say you reaped.

Because you made sacrifices to ensure I am who I am, you were not able to have all the hobbies you may have wanted or the career which could have made you rich. You didn't have the clothes I am sure you desired or cars you admired. No, you sacrificed, and I see it. Anyone reading this book sees it. I am your paycheck and I don't want to be a small one. You deserve to be a billionaire in this respect. I will do my very best to not let you down. I am sorry for when I already have.

So, thank you. They are simple words. Thank you. But you told me to say them, and I am. From the bottom of my heart. I promise to do my best to take these patterns and teach them to Caleb. He can now be another part of your harvest.

I love you,
  Sarah

Chapter Six

Now, was that a success for my mom? You tell me. George, what do you think? Would your mom feel successful if you wrote her a letter like that? I am a mom. I can tell you I would be richer than any king if I received that letter. My mother is a wild success; she is unbelievable. If you ever have the opportunity to meet her, you should feel honored and you should tell her so.

Success!

tool time with tessie

I love my mother. She is one special lady, as you can plainly see. She just told me she wants you to do a bit of work.

P.S. I personally love the fact you are writing in this book. They would not allow us when we were children. I give you permission. You may color outside the lines, too, but **please do not run with a pair of scissors,** your mom was right about that one!

God bless my mom. She gave us many tools and a much needed lunch break. Thanks mom.

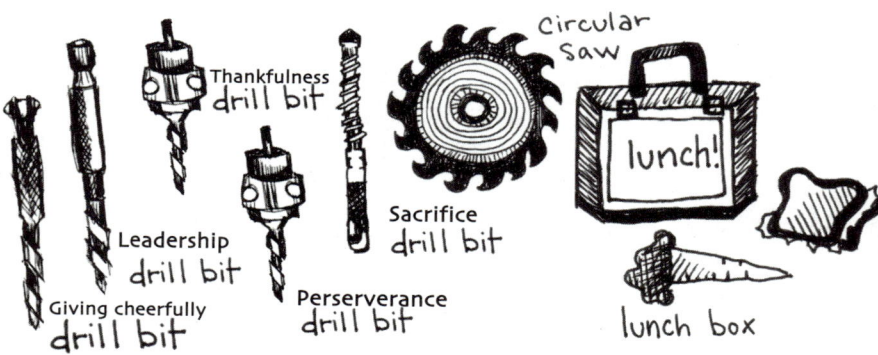

I am actually sad about being able to show only one of her screws.

 **I WILL FINISH THE POTATO SACK RACE!**

I say it like I mean it. Do you feel the need to write your mother a letter?

Find a few screws of your own and place them on your computer at work to begin your day on a positive *note*.

Do not forget the lilies....

Be Still. Hear.

Henry the Rat

Serving others makes you thankful.
Being thankful can make problems disappear.

You did not really think I was going to mention a rat scurrying around our house in Mexico and not tell you a story, did you?

"George, she's telling another story. Get over here," you reply eagerly.

Thank you, I am glad you like them. We need to talk about my mother's other half, dear old dad——awesome, quirky, loving Dad.

My dad burst into the hospital room where my mother is lying. My sister was to be her last child. A hysterectomy insured this and she was recovering. My dad was full of passion and when he made his mind up to do something, well, he did it right then and there. He did not always have a logical plan laid out. Fake it till you make it, was his motto. He was the King of Tap Dancing. Still is. Sound familiar? My mom and I can only bow at his feet.

I suppose this makes me the Princess of Tap Dancing. Ironically, my name means princess. Just thought I would hand you a useless piece of Tessie trivia.

He was always passionate and today was no exception. He was talking a mile a minute and my mom needed another nap. Now that I think of it, the entire family wore out my even-tempered mother.

Chapter Seven

Sorry, Mom. Cannot say we will ever stop. Thank you, God, for naps.

He tells her: "Peggy, God told me to become a pastor and move the whole family to Mexico. Well, first we need to be trained to be missionaries, but we will all be missionaries. We can sell the huge house we just built, and I will not have a "real" job anymore. I sold the nice new car and traded it in for an old station wagon, and rented a U-Haul. We have two weeks to sell everything we own and move! We're going to a place called Bowie, Texas. Never heard of it? Well, you'll see. It's a great place to raise our two little girls. You can take them out of school, home school them and we can kind of wing-it for a while. Aren't you excited about our new super-fabulous-adventure we are about to embark upon?"

CODE BLUE. ROOM 169. CODE BLUE. SHE IS FADING FAST. ROOM 169. STAT! READY. CLEAR. READY. CLEAR. Beep ... beep ... beep ...

Whew, that was a close one, huh? Dad, really now. Let us all say it in unison: "ARE YOU CRAZY? And if you weren't crazy enough with this harebrained 'missionary scheme,' you picked the worst time to tell dear ole Mom. Jeez."

He could have killed her—and then who would have taken me to swim lessons?

Well, the point is, **my dad found his passion, purpose and message, and could not wait to tell the world.** He was ready, and that is an understatement.

paint

Reflects out moods and inspiration. Paint your own design on your life

Problem was, he had to take three of us with him on his journey—three females, no less. Poor Dad. You know he lost a lot of battles along the way. Let's take a moment to feel sorry for him, before we point out all the reasons why we feel even *sorrier* for my mom.

Moment. Okay, done.

Do you know what my mother heard? That positive power drill remained in her toolbox at first. Hey, you would have thrown yours out the window. Trust me. I know you! You too, George.

So, the negative thoughts crept up and I believe she heard this: "Peggy. God told me to quit the job to give you your first new home and car. You are going to be poor again. Let's sell all of the stuff you have been buying and all the keepsakes holding memories of the family we have built. Do this for me, and try to avoid distracting me by having a nervous breakdown."

Chapter Seven

Hey, we *all* would have heard something similar. I will never be hard on her for that. But I have to say, you will now see what I was talking about her being annoying. She picked up her positive power drill, her sacrifice drill bit, her "I help my husband follow his dream" screw, strapped on her tool belt and said, "Let's do it!"

Compromise & Change
Hard to give up your own selfish desires? Strap this bit on and get to drilling!

drill bit

Annoyed, aren't you?

trash can

Throw those negative thoughts and old patterns in the trash

Yes you are, because you know you would not have done it. I am not saying she did not drop the tools now and then. But she always picked them back up. See, my parents were true partners, another pattern. We will talk about that later.

Bowie, Texas. I saw a shirt two years ago which read, "Where the HELL is Bowie, Texas?" I will not tell you. Get a map. Hell is a strong word, but it seemed to fit——a hellhole, you would have called it.

Humor
Laughter is the best medicine

Here is where I tell you laughter is the best medicine. Oh, the stories. When your parents pick up the positive power drill, man, your life is interesting, because you learn to find humor in everything. Even the Bible reads, "a merry heart doeth good like a medicine." So, the family that laughs together—well, they pee their pants, that's what!

Our house. It had two rooms and was on stilts. Goats lived under those rickety stilts. We named them, or should I say my creative mother did. She was always naming possessions, animals, etc, to give them character. Our old cars had names to endear them to us. "Hope" was one. We always *hoped* it would start, etc., and it worked. It made us think positively of those ugly cars. My sister did rename it "Bondo." Fitting name considering the amount of bondo stuck to the side. She even gave it a nick name——"cow pie." Oh Alison, you are just not quite as positive as dear ole mom.
P.S. I secretly liked your names better. Shhhh.

Our friends in high school stole stickers from Taco Bell's windows which read 99¢. They plastered them all over Hope in the middle of the night. We woke up and the whole family laughed. Who cares if our car was old? We knew it, our friends knew it and we laughed about it. They were not being mean and laughing at oneself is a good

Chapter Seven

thing. My mom laughed with us, although she said God would not like the fact they stole.

Aw, Mom. You are too honest.

Okay, so the goats, Lady ... Sunshine ... and Matthew. Most parents would be annoyed goats lived under the house and used their horns to hit the floors and wake them up. I am sure we had our days of cursing those goats, but by naming them, they seemed more like pets and were tolerated. We could not get rid of them; they were wild and we lived in the middle of nowhere. Trust me, this was missionary training. They were training us to go to a Third World country and survive. We might as well find the joy in our situation, and we did.

We had to walk a mile to the bathtub. We had an outhouse. Sunshine liked to lock us in there once in a while. Poor Alison was locked in for roughly an hour. We laughed. Sorry, sis, but it was funny to hear you cry. Sunshine was very smart and we are very mean. He he.

My parents both had great attitudes. Let's make the best of it and make lemonade out of lemons. Paint those patterns yellow! When it was hot, they found a huge horse trough, cleaned it out, put water in it and made a pool for us. There were other families in training and they had young ones. We all used it. My parents were the coolest.

When we walked to the bathhouse, we were never taught to complain about the exercise. In fact, now that I think of it, I never even thought it was a bad thing we were walking. We had fun. My parents made up stories. My dad sang. Boy, could he sing and we looked up at God's stars and I remember the Milky Way, the Big Dipper and the Little Dipper. We were taught to be still and look around us, even then. My parents were handing out important tools to elementary-age children.

Years later, for some reason my dad lost his singing voice. I mean, he was not a star or anything, but he did make a record before he lost it. We loved to listen to it while he was out of town. It made us feel connected to him as he traveled to make money. My father is completely old-school. The songs are old church hymns. He loved to sing and I still enjoy hearing them. The newer stuff can be overrated. You may not agree and you may not enjoy hymns, but at least he sang with passion. We all know by now I did not get his gift, so I appreciate it more. Anyway, he lost his voice and he was down hearted.

Here is what I have decided about that. Dad, God knew if you continued to sing, you would not find your passion for preaching. He needed the speaking part of your voice more than the singing part. You have much to say. Maybe people don't always listen, that is their loss, and trust me, you are a brilliant man. If you want

Chapter Seven

people to hear your old record, well then, in the back of this book I will put a web address where people can send money and buy it. There you go. Listen up, church people. If you like the old stuff, buy this CD. He is not Frank Sinatra or anything, but you will feel closer to God and hear a man sing out his passion, his message. There is something to be said for that. I admire it.

It took a while for us to actually arrive in Mexico. It can be a process raising money and my father worked diligently. He was always someone you could count on to finish whatever he started. Remember? Finish what you start? Sack race? He always had some new idea to start a company to raise money. Seems like God always wanted him to be a missionary, though, just concentrating on that. No one really ever understood him, not really. Talking to God is not something to which many relate.

Now, you can think he is nuts and I give you the right, but I think he is amazing. **When you finally have the luxury of knowing your reason for being on this earth, and you go for it, that is a HUGE success.** People are riddled with fear, not my dad. He had to do what he had to do and we followed. Some people never have one day in their life when they feel the courage to break the mold and just go for it. He had the support of his family. He was a blessed man, a success.

By the time we were finally settled in Mexico, we were teenagers. POOR DAD! It was crazy. I mean, we were the only blonde girls there and we attracted attention; we stood out like sore thumbs and I just said we were *teenagers*. I do not even need to embellish that statement.

My mom took a while to adjust to the marketplaces and how to do things we never had to do before. Shopping for food was an everyday occurrence, there were no preservatives in the food——washing laundry by hand and hanging it on a line——pumping water to the cistern on the roof and waiting for it to heat by a gas furnace. Heck, the pilot light was always out. We gave up and resigned to taking showers during the heat of the day as the sun heated the water, naturally. We *all* learned a new language. It was a culture shock no matter how much you prepare.

Nights were funny. We took out the ole bug spray and had mosquito killing contests. My mom always won. She won everything——very competitive. We sprayed the house, closed all the screens and left for dinner. Notice the lack of air-conditioning. We returned home and were mosquito free, slept in our hammocks and Henry the Rat randomly made appearances.

He was a mouse who lived in our home, and we could never catch him or kill him, so I named him as my parents taught us, Henry. I am not sure why I named him Henry. I drew

Chapter Seven

funny pictures of him with a sombrero and a guitar. He also had one of those Mexican ponchos and a little hammock. He sang Spanish songs. He could sing like I couldn't, and I sent letters from him to my friends. I think they thought the Mexican sun fried my brain. Why didn't I name him a cool Spanish name? Why did I lower his mouse status to a rat? I was weird.

Henry was always there. He became our little mascot. How in the heck my parents made us all happy is beyond me. We were not perfect by any means and did not always have a great attitude. Who does, really? But we loved each other and my dad was doing what he was told to do. I mean, he was a whole other person down there. Back in the USA, he was Mr. Three-Piece Suit. I watched him turn into Jesus or John the Baptist, take your pick. Yeah, I said Jesus. Relax.

A man who would not leave the house without a spit shine, or allow a five o'clock shadow to even think about emerging on his face, was now a wild man. He slept in the villages, wore their style of clothing and bathed in a bucket. He ate like them. His hair became shaggy. He wore sandals—gasp—and five o'clock shadows became a regular occurance. But, man, he was where he was supposed to be and he was happy. He even looked like God's disciple.

Here we are in the villages, helping him and we see a need for a school for the little ones. Can you imagine they have never even seen a crayon? Children you know break them like twigs. These special children held on to them and relished the next time we would come and bring them something. I made them coloring books. Since I love to draw, I made simple ones with the alphabet to teach reading and writing in Spanish. I wish you could have seen their faces when they witnessed their names in print for the first time. I was always tap dancing, doing things I had never done before. We all were. We barely spoke the language and here we were teaching them to write their own language. That was a wonderful success.

My family relates to movie stars traveling to third-world countries to help. What they must feel inside! Actually, I know exactly what they feel and words cannot describe it. They saw what we saw: a child's face discovering a mere crayon while our own children break them. I believe my father gave the same percentage of money they did, comparative to what was in his bank account. I have tears as I now imagine the guts it took for him to do what he did.

Now here is the point of all this. **Serving others made me so incredibly grateful for all I had.** I gave most of my clothes away. Whatever I had, was shared. I loved those nutty people and they loved us. I honestly changed so many of my own patterns down there. Materialism did not have much of a place in our world. Being grateful for what you

Chapter Seven

are given provides you with compassion for others and yourself. I am so grateful to even have been handed that tool at such a young age. Most people do not find one day in their life where there is an opportunity to obtain it. They do not spend even one minute serving and learning. You miss out on blessings if you do not understand service. I see another success.

Let's begin thinking of these little successes as huge successes. Okay? Please do.

Service
Take time to serve mankind

drill bit

My dad has had his ups and downs with being able to stay in Mexico full-time. Sickness, on many of our parts, brought him home time and again. But he was loyal to us. If I was sick with cholera and could not receive proper treatment there, he returned home with me. The home church never understood us, not really. We did not even fit *their* little mold. My dad breaks all molds, ALL MOLDS.

He has his own mission board now and he does what he can. He cannot seem to fit in even the coolest of churches. He is more of a highways and byways kind of guy and I love that. I really admire him. He is real... true blue. What you see is what you get. I am not downing the church. It just was not his purpose to fit into one.

You may sit there and think, well, he did not do anything huge or change a whole nation or anything. But let me tell you, **my father is a wild success.** He is one of the most intelligent men I have encountered. He sacrifices his life for others. Did you notice he never let the work come first when we really needed him? No way, and he took heck for it. He would do anything for his girls.

Loyalty
Stand firm and remain loyal when the tests come

He has shown me love every day of my life. He would never let me feel anything but love and respect for myself. He built me up, showed me what hard work is and how to serve others. He was the example of what to do *after* you find the call on your life, and we all have one.

Can you see, thus far, we have been working toward helping you find yours? By George, I think you are starting to see what our tools could be building. We will get there.

Chapter Seven

My dad is not rich in his bank account. He does not pastor a fancy church with a huge offering every Sunday or have a television show. He is not famous. He sounds a little crazy when you speak to him. He is passionate and he cries when he preaches about his life's work. He proclaims his message. He is loving, kind, funny and sarcastic. I loved having him read to me as a little girl. He would interrupt the Bible stories with his own made-up commercials. Not many people are blessed to see that side of my dad. He seems reserved. He is 70, and still very old-school but I adore him.

Daddy rabbit,

For the record, you are a wild success. You have shown me patterns which will remain with me forever. You have given me tools money cannot buy. Your example of what to expect in a man is priceless and have shown us all what dedication and loyalty are worth. You taught us to be grateful and how to make the best of whatever is thrown our way.

I take the biggest tool of all from you. Serving others. You always told me I would be successful in any job I ever had to do, if I just learned to serve and you are right.

Thank you for always building up the self-esteem of your little girls. Your love means so much. I know the patterns you had to break to behave so intimately with your children.

I thank you here and now. Keep the passion alive. I am your biggest fan. I am proud, very proud of you. You are a success, an unbelievable one.

I know you are a man of few, but wise, words. So I will not sit here and fill you with a lot of fluff. Just know I love you and I am passionate as I am because I'm your daughter. I admire your guts. You have never lived one day in fear. I will support whatever harebrained idea that might come your way for the next 20 years. I'm your kid. Thank you for being my dad.

I love you,
Your Sarah Bear

Chapter Seven

"George, I think this girl must have married a man just like her daddy," you say.

Umm, okay. We need to chat.

Remember the whole man-pattern I was screwing up? Remember the scars on my face, but I told you of the ones you could not see? Like the ones on my heart? Something happened to me when I was about 22 that sat me on my @$$, and shook me up. It took all the self-righteousness out of me.

Um. Yeah. I did not quite marry a man like my dad. Well, in a way he was or they were. Yup. Two marriages. Two divorces. Here we go. Take a nap before I get started on this one!

tool time with tessie

I miss Henry. My renderings of him made me laugh often. In fact, I smile when I think of my family's time in Mexico and I continue to spend my time there. Well, you know it is time to get to work. Ready?

paint

Finding the tools is beginning to seem like a scavenger hunt of sorts. What did we find? Paint brush and paint, trashcan, and you guessed it, more drill bits.

trash can

Humor drill bit

Loyalty drill bit

Service drill bit

drill bit
Compromise & Change

My dad gives us one of my favorite screws:

SERVING OTHERS CREATES GRATITUDE IN ME

Take time to serve another person. You will be rewarded in ways money cannot buy.

Pick up your journal and pen and find a few screws of your own. Hey, you could even draw a picture of a "rat" in your own life. Give thankfulness a try.
I will be taking a quick nap.

Be Open. Give.

Don't Flush the Toilet, Buy a New One

Y ou require balance in your life.
Being too extreme will waste your time.

To tell you about the man I first chose, I must give you a little background. I know, *more background.* Be patient. You know the whole type A thing? Well, I have to tell you, both my grandparents were very anal. My dad was, too. Yes, me as well. My little, precious Caleb? Yup, perfectionist already. He is three and I have yet to clean his room.

"I think she is a fibber," says George.

It is true. He will not let me. He can do it better and all by himself. He is a mini-me. What can I say? A little background on my grandparents will shed light on everything.

Before I even begin, I want to make one thing clear. I loved my grandparents very much. We were close. They were of the Great Depression era, frugal and strict. Back then, men did men stuff and women did women stuff. I will tell a few stories to make a point, but I need to show a few, this time, which do not paint such a healthy picture. I will absolutely praise them too, do not worry. I will end with showing you how they broke patterns later in life. It is never too late, people, never——just like my mother's mom.

Now, on to the story. I love you, Grandma and Grandpa, but they need to hear about your nutty, anal ways. It is just good comedy.

My grandparents made sure everything was always perfect in

Chapter Eight

their house. Everything had its place. Each figurine had a special spot. My grandma loved the whole figurine collecting thing. Every antique was polished, bathrooms were spotless and a squeegee hung from each shower wall. We were expected to, as their guest, wipe down the wall after we showered. If we failed to do so, my grandma would become upset, cry and complain to my father how her ungrateful grandchildren did not wipe them down and therefore, left her with more work to do. That was not very nice, she said and was not thoughtful. I remember thinking I was a thoughtful child, but Grandma did not think so. In fact, she seemed to think everything I did was not really all that great.

"Grandma. Let me tell you how we won our cheerleading competition!" I would say.

"Oh, honey, back in my day …" she'd reply.

The ending was always the same. Those three dots are a filler until you heard, "and that is why it was better in my day."

It used to hurt my feelings, a lot. I assumed she did not like me and did not think I could do anything right. She always took the opposite view on everything, any topic. Whatever you want to throw at her, I could tell you in a hundred words or less, what my grandma would have said. It would take using my "be still" lunch break, to one day find a light bulb and shed light on why she did this. Trust me, she was a wise woman with much to say. I did not get it yet— too young and not conscious whatsoever.

The house was orderly. The beds must be made or we could not leave the room. We even had to put our blankets back in big vacuum-sealed bags daily. Really. Coffee cans were saved and lined with Ziploc baggies. We were to only put banana peels in there. "Banana peels only," it should have read. Please do not forget to put the lid on. Two reasons for that. Number one: Putting them with the rest of the trash caused the house to smell. Number two: She said she was respectful of all people, even the trash man. He has a difficult job and she did not like to think of him having the smelly trash dumped all over him. We were always helping my grandparents dust. Cool thing about all this was, when you visited, at least you could always find what you needed. It was always right there, where it was a year ago.

One night, we were sleeping over at their house and my mom got up to use the bathroom in the middle of the night, as many of us do. I mean, she had to pee. She did what she needed to and did not want to wake us up as she tiptoed down the hall. She is thoughtful and decided it was not a good idea to flush the toilet; it was only pee after all. No big deal, right? I mean, we have all done it, left it so the actual flushing would not wake anyone up.

Chapter Eight

"What a sweet lady, George, always thinking of others," you are saying with a smile.

I know she is. Problem was, my grandparents were perfectionists—**times 100!** They probably would have been diagnosed with obsessive-compulsive disorder, had it been the thing to do "back in their day."

I woke up to my grandfather screaming. I mean, he was not scary when he screamed, he just screamed about stuff in a tantrum-like voice.

"Sis" (his pet name for my grandma). "Right in our own family! Can you believe it?" he ranted.

What in the world, I wondered. What was "right in our own family?" What?

"Someone right in our own family peed in the toilet and left it there, ALL NIGHT."

Uh-oh. I knew how anal they were about their house. Someone was in trouble and all I knew was it was not me. My mom fessed up and told them why. He walked off in a huff. My grandma was in shock my mom did that, mortified. It was a very quiet day. I think a lot of polishing of furniture was accomplished in the subsequent hours.

Here is where I just cannot believe I am about to write this and print it.

Because you will say, "George, this girl does seem to fib. She exaggerates and sucks me into these stories. I am not gonna listen to them anymore."

level

Having balance in our life is the level

Okay, yes, sometimes I add a little dramatic flair to the story, but I do not change the facts, not one bit. I *promise* you, **my grandfather had that toilet REMOVED!** He tore it out and put in a new one... *all because pee was left there overnight!*

There are so many lessons in that paragraph it makes my head spin. My grandfather was not balanced. He was extreme. I think balancing ourselves out should now be a tool. Let's make it a level. Sound good to you, George? How about you? What do you think?

He did not use his level, did he? Because he was obsessed with things being his own way, he allowed himself to get all worked up. He tore out something which did not need to be removed; it only needed to be cleaned a little.

Chapter Eight

Put down the sledgehammer, Grandpa. Jeez.

Look what he did to my mom. This belittled her and made her feel small. She did not mean to cause such a ruckus. In fact, she was trying everything *not* to cause one. That was the point of what she did. She was thinking of others and being respectful of our sleep. Grandpa was the one who woke us up yelling and ranting, about something so trivial. But because he was not balanced and had not ever used his level when building steps, he did not view them as trivial. It was obviously so big of a deal, he went to the store, bought a new toilet, tore up the old one and installed a brand-new commode.

Have I stopped to ponder the amount of time it took for him to do that? Yes, I have. What a waste of his energy. He put his energy into something negative. It wasted all of his day and a negative step was built, one I am not sure was ever broken. Honestly, I think it is a pattern I finally broke. Two complete generations later and it even took me years. Let us all pray Caleb is somewhat normal, shall we?

Grandpa could have handled it *so* differently. By using a sponge and some soap to clean the toilet, he would not have wasted the day doing that. Think about what he missed. What could he have accomplished? Can you imagine what we are missing when we do this to ourselves? We all do it.

I will tell you later how I have given up an entire day with negative thinking and responding. I did stop to think of what I was missing, something very important. It pains me to this day to realize how reacting instead of making conscious choices has caused me to miss out. We will get to that.

Do you react to life? Or are you proactive? Do you react to people? Or do you make conscious choices?

I am beginning to see how making choices and becoming a conscious person is pretty much gonna be the whole point of this book.

light bulb

"How do you do that?" you ask.

We are getting closer.

He could have chosen not to speak negatively to my mother, by using his positive power drill. She beat herself up a bit for it and it tore her down in front of us. We saw this behavior and it entered our tiny minds. We were sent the message it was acceptable to correct the daughter-in-law in front of everyone and she was forced to take it, in stride. Watch what you teach your grandchildren. Trust me, they are listening. I was listening. We will get to what I heard in Chapter 9.

Chapter Eight

I tell you all of this, not to pick on my dear grandparents, but to point out they were dropping a very important tool. I did not see it until later. Can you guess what it was? I cannot tell you yet. I will, however, give you a hint. It is one we all need to break patterns.

"Remind me to tell you, George. Okay? You have a job to do."

They were awesome people, brilliant, a little stern, but loving. I used to love it as they stood in their driveway and waved goodbye to us when we left. They stood there until we were out of sight. We loved going for rides on Grandpa's golf cart. He took us to see the Christmas lights around the neighborhood. They were kind people, to everyone.

I am not going to go into all the details of their life. It would be inappropriate and I do not have permission, but I do need to tell you they were very successful in the world's eyes. They made a lot of money as business owners. My dad tried to fit into their mold for a while. He was married, then divorced. He tried to work for my grandfather, but left the business. He and my grandfather both drank heavily which caused health problems down the road. They both broke those patterns though, on two different paths, but they did it. Way to go, Dad and Grandpa! What a success.

Success!

My dad walked out of it, I mean all of it, when he was in his thirties. He remarried, this time to my nutty mom and the rest is history. I mean, she is such a pattern break it is not even funny. She is nothing like his mother or ex-wife. She breaks all molds. He never drank again. He never went back into conventional business. He had mission work to do. He had a message to spread and my mom loved him all those years, still does. He still chases her around the house. It makes me smile. It should gross me out, but nah, I want that. I want a man to chase me around when he is 70, look at me with wonder and write me love notes. He is a good-looking man, kind. My parents are pretty darn cool, I must say.

My grandpa took a while longer. Eventually, the work and poor health patterns caught up and he suffered strokes, several of them. I believe he was forced to change. In fact, he told me so. He said God woke him up.

Wake-up call time. He'd tell you the same thing. He said he was glad it happened——the strokes I mean. They forced him to be still and listen, to hear God. See, I think we all need to pay attention to that. Why don't we just break the patterns now? C'mon. Let's not wait for wake-up calls. Those pretty much stink.

light bulb

He was forced to learn to read and write all over again and Grandma taught him. They finally spent quality time together. Work was no longer priority. He was obsessed with

Chapter Eight

the business his entire life but now, they sat and talked, learning together in those later years. She sat by his side. He would become frustrated and she patiently helped him. They were the perfect team.

He became softer too. He said, "I love you," much more often. He talked about God, so did she. My dad taught his parents about God, really. My parents both gave this Light to their parents. Interesting, huh? They loosened up a bit. Still had all the little things we had to do, but they did calm down and they taught us much.

Remember the trash man? I want to point out she dropped the respect tool. My grandparents, with all their money, taught me everyone was important and deserved respect. She loved her trash man, the mailman and the housekeeper she employed when she aged. We were taught to love ourselves, but we were to never think of ourselves higher than anyone. We were all the same, but different, remember? This carried over into my experiences in Mexico. I was taught equality.

Self Respect
Hold your head high, but do not look down upon others

drill bit

They sharpened their minds by talking about the good ole days. I know that now. Remember when I said I thought Grandma did not like me? Grandma was not putting down

my accomplishments, she was keeping her mind intact. Turns out she had a fear of developing Alzheimer's. I was not listening or connecting to that idea. Talking about the past or debating my ideas kept her mind active and exercised. I am glad I finally did connect to it, though. It made my relationship with her so much stronger.
I loved them.

light bulb

When they would sit and tell us how God kept them together, as partners, it made me smile. They died loving each other after almost 65 years of marriage. They died loving us and God. They loved my dad and they really loved my mother. She finally won them over and was by their side until their last breaths. They were buried together. It was all planned out by them, perfectionists to the bitter end. God bless them both, they gave me so much.

So, we will now jump to husband number one. Let's call him David, shall we? I told you all of *that* so you would be able to see why I was attracted to my ex-husband. Because when we get into the next chapter, you will say, "What the heck fire? Why in the world would lil Miss Happy In This World pick *THAT* guy?"

Chapter Eight

Here we go.

You are
not going to be very proud
of me, George.

tool time with tessie

WOW! Throwing away an entire toilet is pretty extreme, huh? I hope you had a good laugh. My family is always laughing and maybe you can see why. But, alas, we must get to work now.

My dear grandparents handed us a level and an other drill bit.

level

Self Respect drill bit

The screw for balancing out our lives is:

 **I HAVE COMPASSION WITH MYSELF**

I say this to myself as I look in the mirror, and smile.

I need to be prepared to assist Caleb when the type A personality really begins to take hold. He is the best thing I have ever done and I love handing him tools. I hope you are writing along with me! What is your screw?

Have you ever wasted a day with negative behavior?

Be Balanced. Love.

Sleeping With the Enemy

Some commitments must be broken.
Having the strength to, is the challenge.

She opens her cabinets. They are well organized. The canned vegetables are in one line, the fruit in another. All labels face forward. The refrigerator is equally as organized. The ketchup is placed beside the mustard, because it would make no sense to be next to the jelly. She is cautious to always make sure everything is in its proper place. She would not want to incur his wrath.

She moves into the closet and hangs his newly starched shirt in its special place. Everything is arranged according to color and style—long sleeves with long sleeves, short sleeves with short. She has learned the hard way what can happen when the starch is not up to his standards or the shirts are out of their logical order. He becomes angry.

He has a temper and she does not want to upset him. She does not answer her sister's call as the phone rings. He does not approve of her talking to her own family. He is possessive. She looks longingly at the phone, but returns to her chores.

She drinks her skim milk and dresses in her workout clothes. She cannot risk getting fat. He would not like that. She is very careful about her appearance. She has whitened her teeth and is pressured to wear braces on her slightly crooked, lower ones. Actually, she is careful about everything. The towels in the sparkling bathroom are lined up just so. They have to be even, must be even. She changes

Chapter Nine

the toilet paper roll and makes sure it faces outward for easier use.

She dusts the nightstand. She is careful with the gun in there; it scares her. She has been warned it has no safety. It is there in case anyone might want to do them harm. She wonders what would protect her if he discovered the mistakes she made throughout her day. Every day is a walk on an endless mile of eggshells. Her self-esteem is shot. She only knows what he thinks of her now. What she thinks of herself is no longer important. What a sad person.

"George, I don't like the beginning of this chapter very much. She is usually pretty funny. This is not funny," you are saying.

I know it isn't. I am sorry to depress you, but the story needs to be told. This was me at age 22, married to David. A man with whom I fell in love, married and eventually left.

Now, this is not a book about abuse, per se. I am not here to act as your therapist, if you are in an abusive marriage or relationship. I am not going to delve into the gory details of what he did to me and what I allowed him to do. I think you can pretty much figure it out. But I am going to tell you, right now, **the only answer is to LEAVE. Plain and simple.**

YOU MUST LEAVE.

You will find resources at the end of this book for help. Okay? Trust me, I know how hard it is to leave and I am of the belief it cannot be done alone.

Other than that, we are going to talk about how I left and what I gained from all of this. Yup, that is right, positive power drill to the rescue. I am actually glad I married him and had that near-death experience, sure am. Hey, give me a break. I talk to guardrails. I am a fruitcake. You should know by now I am the type of person who can be grateful she lived through such an ordeal.

By the way, he *was* right about the toilet paper; it should always face out. Nope, would not change a thing. Well, maybe one. Skim milk pretty much blows!

I did not live this way for very long, thank God. Some people out there have it so much more difficult than I did. I stayed for only one year. But I have to admit, that is only because my mom "kidnapped" me when she found out what was going on. The only reason it was not my dad who kidnapped me is simple. If David had been at the house when he arrived, my dad would be on death row.

I am sure you can imagine what my father must have felt. He would never treat me this way. We never saw anything

Chapter Nine

like that. If it weren't for my parents, I do not believe I would have had the inner strength to leave. Unless you have experienced any type of abuse, you cannot possibly understand how weak you become.

So, what the heck happened to cause me to pick this guy? Well, like most relationships, it starts out hidden. I mean, I do not know any women in that situation who says their man came up to them on the first date and said, **"Hey, you will be under my full control or I will harm you. Allow me to drag you off to my cave by your hair. You are no longer allowed to think for yourself."** It just does not happen that way.

He was incredibly charming and I fell in love at first sight. I met him at my work. He was a successful engineer. His parents disapproved right away. One was a surgeon and one a psychiatrist. I did not finish college. I had come back from Mexico, began a career in apartment management and was working toward starting my own business. I was bored in school. I had the highest of SAT scores, but I grew tired of learning "in theory." I was ready to get on with life. No matter how much I tried to prove otherwise, to them, I was stupid. In fact, anyone without a college degree was.

Sorry, all you awesome, famous people with no degree, who improve lives daily…you are officially stupid, according to them. But I allowed them to treat me badly——my first mistake.

Remember I said I sort of saw this with my mom and grandparents? It was less extreme, but having in-laws who did not approve, did not seem odd to me. I witnessed the fact my grandparents came to love my mom as a daughter. I naturally assumed I would win them over. Yeah——didn't happen.

His abuse began more slowly. Little by little, he did the opposite of what my parents taught me. Remember we talked about not putting others down to make yourself look better? Well, that was not David. Putting others down was his hobby. Slowly but surely, he gained control over me and whittled away at my healthy self-esteem.

See, in the beginning I thought I was marrying the same type of man as my grandpa or my dad. Everything was orderly and clean, like Grandpa's house. Dad was raised that way and he had a temper from time to time and raised his voice. No big deal. We were loved. We ended up laughing at the anal stuff. Even my dad would laugh at himself when he became too rigid. We would howl at my grandparents' anal ways. They made us shake our heads. That is what I assumed it would be like with David.

Boy, was I ever wrong!

Chapter Nine

Do you understand why I told you about my grandparents? A whole chapter was dedicated simply for you to relate to where I was coming from. See, it seemed okay to me he was rigid——kind of normal.

I must say here and now, my sister Alison saw through him. She disliked him and even refused to be my maid of honor. My best friend in the world did not stand up for me at our wedding. Duffy had abandoned Tessie. I mean, could there have been any more red flags for me to see?

No one else saw it and we all told Ali to pipe down and support my happiness. She even said he reminded her of the movie, *Sleeping with the Enemy*. We all brushed her off, and I married him. Oh my. Yup. Saved my whole body for this guy. What a gift to give, huh? Do not think it was appreciated very much, do you?

My grandparents and parents did not teach me all of this. They were rigid, but no one was physically hurt for it. No one was actually afraid of my father's hand or their yelling. We just laughed days later about their little rants. They could get so worked up over nothing. We teased them and they bore it. They were well aware of their flaws and hey, I was a bit of a

light bulb cover

For those "red flags" that keep knocking out our light

yeller at times. I got worked up. But now, getting worked up was his job. I learned to be quiet very fast.

I finally left after some major events unfolded. Okay, my mom **forced** me to leave. I do not think giving you full detail is what you need right now. This is about what I learned, not what crippled me as a human. I lived with my parents and hid out for a while and I remember the day I finally woke up. I mean, I still wanted to go back to him. I had become so small I could not imagine doing anything on my own. My light that once shone so brightly, had been completely snuffed out by a man. **Do you want to know what woke me up?** A car ride.

I was sitting in my mother's new truck. They were back from Mexico for a while and they began a landscape business to get by, until the next round of trips. We had not had new things since Dad decided to do mission work and I knew she loved her truck. Well, I spilled tea all over the front carpet by knocking over the cup. I freaked out, cried and tried to clean it up. I apologized over and over and told her not to harm me. I hid on one side of the truck, sobbing, as if it were the end of the world. It was first-grade all over again. I was in torment. She swerved the truck to a halt on the side of the road. I thought I was gonna get it.

light bulb

Chapter Nine

You know what she did? No, not a nap this time, not even a hug right away. She took the cup and dumped what tea was left in it, all over the floor and seats—just kept dumping it. She grabbed me and had me watch. She held me down and forced a hug on me and told me she loved me, even when I screwed up, just like the spelling test. Then she let me sob. The flood gates opened as she rubbed my hair, my face. She wiped my tears, put both her hands around my cheeks and said, "I don't ever want to see you act like that again, young lady. Do you hear me? I didn't raise you to hate yourself. **You will love yourself again if it is the last thing I do.**"

Getting another, healthy helper is necessary at times

Thank God I had this type of parents. Trust me, my dad was there too. Oh, he was there making sure I was safe. He could not talk about it as much because, frankly, he was plotting the perfect murder, I believe. Like how could he kill my ex-husband and not get caught. Part of that is a joke, but I know it enters the minds of parents when someone hurts their child, especially the way David did.

I want to say something else. The ironic thing is, his parents, the surgeon and psychiatrist, blamed me! I had the poor little, misfit family and he had this wealthy, well-educated fortress of a family. His incredible abuse was somehow my fault. I know I provoked Alison and Ben, but we joked. A little hit to the stomach in elementary school is not a huge deal, but what *he* did was unimaginable.

Now, who do you think were the stupid ones? I would not trade my poor, little, misfit family for 100 of his. I had to get that off my chest. But I need you to make a mental note of what I am saying. Parents who would blame that on me obviously were not very close to their son. Sure they spoke, but there was an obvious disconnect there. I did not realize this pattern was beginning to creep into my already unhealthy man pattern. We will revisit that thought, I promise.

I was forced to never repeat one pattern, though, the one of never being with an anal retentive, abusive man. Actually, being with anyone anal retentive in any way is a turnoff now, abusive or not. I would rather live with a slob. I have never been with a man with a temper again. I promise, not like that.

My parents could only take me so far; the rest was up to me. I became strong … very strong. I made the choice to love myself again. I refused to put braces on my lower teeth. I did not obtain a college degree as he tried to force me to do. I did not allow myself to believe I was stupid and I started my own business. We will get to that, more tap dancing.

Chapter Nine

I was determined to do something for myself, stand on my own two feet and believe in *me* again. With God's guidance and counseling, it all did come flooding back. I believe strongly in healthy counseling, therapy, life coaches—whatever you want to call them. They assisted me in rescuing myself. Use them, people. Let the ego go and seek help. Even finding help is a choice, so we must pick a helper with healthy patterns. How can you know? We will get to that too. Trust me, I understand how a so-called therapist can take advantage. We must always be aware. Everything we do is a choice.

hammer & nails

For the helper to build something very special

What did I learn? So much. I changed the pattern that was passed down, of being too rigid. My perfectionism was beginning to wane. I began to have a lot of compassion for others. Remember I said I could become self-righteous? Well, not anymore. We all travel through the valleys. We all make "horrible choices." It is part of living.

I could have married another abusive man just like him. That is what many people do, keep repeating the same mistakes over and over. Not me, not on this one.

I began to love people and all their problems. I was tainted now, not so shiny and that was okay. I coached a girl through leaving a relationship a year later. I never would have been able to relate to her in any way, had I not been through that.

That is a success! Some people never have one day in their life when they help another through a crisis. They have not chosen to see the positive in their dark situation and they wander through life always being helped and never helping. Trust me, the helping part, feels really good. It is a blessing. I have now joined a mentor program to assist women going through the pains of divorce.

Success!

I said we will get to how to choose the right people when you need help, and we will. That is a whole other ball of wax, a toughie. So often we tend to find the negative ones, don't we? Do not worry, I am going to make it pretty easy for you. Well, that is *if* I do my job as a writer.

Dangit, I have never written a book before. I cannot even claim a really dynamic essay. I do not have any degrees that could support my being a writer. What am I going to do? More tap dancing, I guess. I will figure it out. You should know by now, I have a way of doing that. We will get there.

I learned something else—big lesson. Letting go of ego.

Chapter Nine

Trust me, perfectionists have egos, so of course I had one. To even tell my mom was a huge step for me. Also, to be little miss perfect with her perfect little life, and have this sort of thing end her marriage, was embarrassing. People were watching. To admit I failed, big-time, was hard to bring into the open for all to see. It took a while for me to see I could not live my life beating myself up over this failure, or any failure, for that matter. **Remember, allowing yourself to fail is a success.** I will stand by that statement. But don't you see? Leaving, overcoming ego, recovering, rebuilding etc. ALL of that is a success. So tell me, why woud I choose to dwell on the "failure?" In fact, I have pretty much erased the word *fail* from my vocabulary.

I found a new strength, one of a woman. **I love being a woman.** I do not think I am above a man, but I am not lower, either. Being a strong woman is powerful and I gained most of my power back, but not all. While I did not choose a man like David again, I still had not broken one poor pattern we have been talking about until now—allowing myself to be viewed through a man's eyes and believing I had to fit his mold somehow. Why could I not break it?

Well, why can't you break yours? Could it be we are not seeing what the pattern really is? We will get to that,

blind fold

For re-training your brain

learning to locate patterns. You cannot change what you do not know to change. That is what counselors and books are for, right?

I hope, by the time this book ends, we will have shown you how to retrain your brain to see the patterns. Am I going to have to give you a patch? No, but I will give you a blindfold. For now, hold on to it. You will need it.

Now, what if I had decided to react to this situation as so many do?

Oh, I will never recover from this. Look at what he did to me. I did not deserve this. What if it happens again? I am afraid and now, look at me. I do not even own my own car and he took all my money. What if he comes and finds me? I do not know what to do. Maybe I will just cry and sweep it all under the rug, pretend it didn't happen, unless it is time to use it as an excuse not to act. I will neither ask why, nor will I learn from what happened so I can prevent this from occurring again. I will live in fear. Maybe I will just stay right here with my parents, indefinitely. They will protect me. I am only 22. This would be acceptable, right?

Chapter Nine

Listen, I know that sounded harsh. I mean, are those "normal" reactions? Did I have those same thoughts? Sure did! If you have escaped out of a similar situation or are thinking about it, you will have these thoughts. You may even turn those thoughts into action.

But I began to learn I cannot go around life reacting. That would simply do me no good. "Normal" reactions are not acceptable behavior. Behavior becomes pattern. I began to learn to make choices in their place. We will definitely be talking about how important that word is … CHOICE. You can make healthy ones or unhealthy ones. Again, your choice.

"Aw, man. Does this mean we're going to have to start thinking?" George whines.

Yup.

Now, what tool did I mention earlier that my grandparents were giving me? Remember, I told you I would revisit the thought? Hmmm. David gave it to me too, so did my dad.

"George, you were supposed to remind her!" you exclaim.

Give him a break. I do not think he was expecting this story. So I will tell you.

They gave me a magnifying glass!

For looking closer to find the patterns

Trust me, we need it. How can we locate patterns we cannot see, unless we have a magnifying glass? We must begin looking closer, analyzing and looking for clues. But we need to be careful with this one, because you can abuse it as David did, or even my granddad and my father did at times.

If you hold a magnifying glass over an object too long in the light, well, it can burn, can't it?

Remember the little boys who would burn ants while allowing the sun to shine through? Do not keep it under the light too long, you can harm yourself, or maybe worse, someone else——or you might throw away a perfectly good toilet!

I also want to warn you how difficult it can seem to use the magnifying glass, at first. When you hold it over your life, you begin to see things about yourself that may not look pretty. In my experience, I was forced to take responsibility for events I previously believed were not my problem. This tends *not* to be very fun. You may even discover poor patterns you were *not* searching for and this can be disheartening. Remember what I said, do not hold it over your life under the light for too long. Okay?

Chapter Nine

Know when to put it down and resume when you are ready again. It truly is a process and we will continue to discuss it over the remainder of the book.

Caleb came into the house last week, crying as I was bringing groceries out of the car. I mean, he was bawling and seemed ashamed, afraid to talk to me. I asked him what was wrong and he kept repeating, "I spill the red. I spill the red." Okay. He is upset about the red? OH! His red drink. He took me by the hand, led me to my new truck and cried. He buried his face in my legs and I saw his fruit punch all over the carpet.

Ironically, it is the same type truck my mother owned when I spilled the tea. Well, he was very ashamed. I picked him up, assured him it was okay, wiped his tears and showed him love. Accidents happen and he should neither feel afraid to tell me, nor act ashamed. I love him even when he makes mistakes.

I told him we could call the Cleaning Prince and he would come take all the juice out of the carpet, like magic. I jumped on the phone and called our mobile detail guy. He came right away, luckily, and extracted the punch. Caleb finally quit crying and smiled. "He fixed it! He fixed it!"

I am so glad he spilled that punch.

It reminded me of my mom and how strong she was with me, yet how kind and loving at the same time. I showed the same love and strength to Caleb. Even when he fails or messes up, he can always feel safe to tell me. It is never too early to contribute to that pattern of his. In fact, I can't afford *not* to.

I highly encourage you to do the same for your children. I feel if he is ever in danger, he will let go of ego and call me as I called my mom that day. Do you see how that story came full circle for me? The spelling test? An "F" in marriage? The tea? Caleb and the punch? Are you beginning to see "what goes around, comes around" … "full circle"… "reap what you sow" … call it what you want, but it does happen. I am proof of it.

light bulb

We will start putting all of this together. We are already doing it actually, building steps along the way. These new healthy patterns are being set one on top of another. I cannot wait until we get to break out the sledgehammer and kill this man pattern of mine. I bet you will help me. It will be fun!

Chapter Nine

Have you ever been angry enough that breaking something up with a sledgehammer would be a great release? Yeah. That is why I love this book. I am going to let you grab hold and pound away.

Let us go ahead and skip all the guys in between and get to husband number two. ¡Numero dos! Man, this is not as much fun as it started out to be, is it? Not for me, at least. Discussing my successes as a little girl was just so darned cute and tons more fun.

George, you haven't said much lately. You still there?

tool time with tessie

I am glad I was able to share my experience with you. Did I inspire you to get to work? That was my intention!

I want to point out something very important to you. This chapter depicts the darkest moment of my life and yet we gained more tools from it than any experience you will find in this book. Do you see how this can be true in your own life? We were also able to find help along the way by enlisting the assistance of a healthy minded person. Let's recap the tools we located.

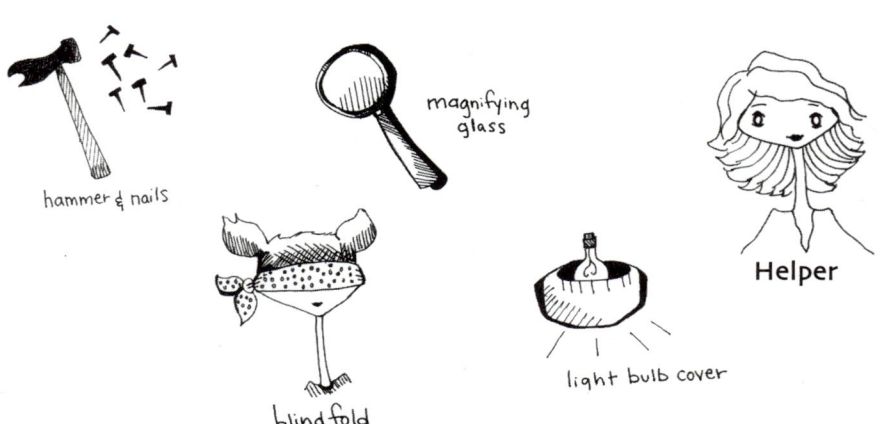

hammer & nails

magnifying glass

blind fold

light bulb cover

Helper

You will not believe how many screws we found, but I can only give you one.

I AM NOT BROKEN AND I WILL NOT ACCEPT ANYONE WHO TELLS ME I AM!

I love to say this out loud several times per day. Talking to myself is empowering.

**Write and stand in your own power.
I encourage it!**

Be Strong. Survive.

Don't Throw Darts

Being a conscious person means making choices. Reacting to life just won't cut it.

Let's head back to the health resort in Tuscon, Arizona, 2006.

The retreat provides a menu of services to help just about any sort of person. There are medical professionals and holistic ones. Priests and clairvoyants. Fitness programs for any level and an entire yoga/martial arts program. The food is amazing, fresh and healthy. Movie stars enjoy this facility for several reasons. They train physically for movies, beat addictions or simply relax. I have already described the locker room so you can only imagine what the actual spa entails. Have I been very fortunate to enjoy this oasis on several occasions? Absolutely, and am the better for it, truly grateful. The tools I acquired are priceless.

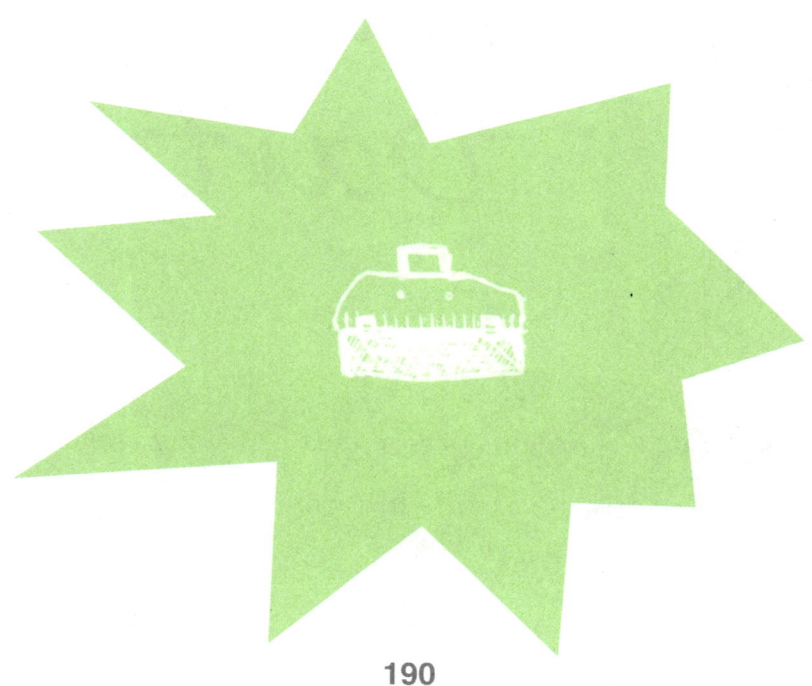

Chapter Ten

I had just signed off on papers for my second divorce. This one was much different. We have a precious three-year-old boy and one cannot really "end it" when there is a child involved. So I am here, trying to obtain tools to assist me in raising a child alone and somehow find a way NOT to put him in the middle. You see the majority doing it. I needed ideas on how to deal with his feelings of abandonment, which have plagued him all year. I watch and listen to people. Remember the cold dip pool story? This was the same trip. I began writing here, observing and learning. I was not in need of help for me, per se; this was more about my child. So I thought.

WHEN YOU HAVE A CHILD, IT IS NEVER OVER

A van met me and a couple from New York at the airport. The ride to the ranch is about 45 minutes and I began to notice their behavior. This couple was celebrating their 25th wedding anniversary, but something did not seem right. She complained he was on the phone all day as they traveled. She was not nagging him; she seemed genuinely hurt. What I heard was: "You are not here with me." He was supposed to be there with her but all he did was sit on his phone with work, or his buddies and talk about the game.

She was excited, opened up her handbook and began talking about what she wanted to do and try. She seemed eager to connect to him. She was choosing activities involving the two of them, growth classes. He ignored his book and threw it on the seat. He paid no attention when she spoke. He was a doctor—— very important man. He did not hold her hand. He answered every phone call.

I could feel their energy and they were not connected. They seemed distant, as if they led different lives. I have seen them at dinner, in the spa, etc. Her eyes appear lonely and he is preoccupied. We are not permitted to use cell phones in common areas, so he would leave dinner to answer his texts.

I know it has been 25 years for them, and so many believe time does this to couples. I believe I can have what my parents enjoy, yet I cannot help but think ... that would have been me! Had I continued in my passionless marriage, this would have been me in 18 years. I do not ever want to go away again and spend my energy, money and time, and feel that sad and lonely... or feel that disconnected to someone with whom I was going away for one purpose—to connect! That has already been me. I know the hurt in her eyes. Everything else seemed more important to him than she was.

light bulb

Here I was, going for tools to help Caleb, and old hurts were being brought up for me. Guess I had more work to do. I had been working for one year already. I thought it was

Chapter Ten

over. I mean, we separated *a year ago*. What was the big deal? I had been to counseling, done my yoga, had Reiki, prayed, read books, sought counsel with wise people, had a life coach, etc. **Why were old hurts coming up?**

The answer became obvious. When you have a child in any relationship, unless one parent signs off all contact with the child, it is never over. I mean, never, and those words hit me. Watching that couple behaving distant and unloving reminded me of my marriage. I could not escape these reminders so easily, because I had to see this man every time he came to pick up our little man. Heavy thought: 18 more years of reminders. That did not sound like fun to me.

Maybe you have been through this, and you know this but never truly connected to the idea: It is never over. To look at that sentence on paper is difficult and to take a look at yourself and admit a failure, is outrageously hard. It would be incredibly easy for me to sit here and tell you and myself, it was all him. I did nothing. He worked so much and forgot about me. I dried up. His lack of love dried me up. His drive for success replaced his love for a family unit. I could say all of those things, and I could live every day believing he will "get his judgment," go on with life and lie to myself.

light bulb

In fact, he made it easy for me to say those words, he said them himself. He took all the blame and he even told this to our counselor. But when a marriage falls apart, it always takes two. So I cannot lie to myself. What good would that do? One day I would end up telling that lie to my son and I do not want to do that.

"George, I like it when she can admit she's wrong," you may say.

Thanks! Me too. It is called being humble. I should do it more often.

Once again, I am not going into the gory details of what happened in the marriage. We were both at fault and I was no angel. I will, however, talk about the patterns I continued to keep. I want to share with you how I finally saw the connections between both husbands, and the part I played in the process of ending both marriages. My poor patterns finally came to light. But guys, I chose to take out that magnifying glass. It is not easy. It is harder to fess up, look closely and weep over what you have done wrong, but there is hope.

When you do this—as hard as it is—all bitterness disappears. You move on. You let go. You break down the step and have a fresh opportunity to create a new one. You want an easy fix, don't you, George? Isn't that the

Chapter Ten

American way? Take a pill. Get plastic surgery. Try to lose 50 pounds in one weekend. No one wants to do the work.

·Well, if you want to keep reading, I promise you, you will see, I worked. I will encourage you to work as well. I did finally take out the magnifying glass to look at my man patterns at the age of 33! Three cheers for Sarah!! Hip, hip—okay, that is corny.

> **DO NOT PUT YOUR CHILD IN THE MIDDLE.**
> **I BEG OF YOU, DO NOT DO IT**

What happened? How did I do it again? Getting an *F* in marriage, I mean. First off, I want you to know I love Derek very much. I will always love him. We have a child together and I am a loving person. I do not feel for him as man and wife, but a love is there because I choose for it to be. He should be shown kindness and care, absolutely.

Caleb should be taught to honor his father, love him and to show him respect. How can I teach him these principles, if I do not love him myself? If I do not respect him? Wouldn't that be impossible? So many of you shy away from the word love, when speaking of your ex.

There are many forms of the word and several ways to express it, at least that is how I see it.

So, ladies ... gentlemen ... products of a nasty divorce ... listen up. Because when we are angry and hurtful, we only hurt these innocent children. Then, what is the next generation going to be like? C'mon, let's talk here. It is a process, though. **Allow me to tell you about something I did and boy, was it ever wrong.**

Derek and I separated. Hey, I mean everyone handles that in a different way. It was harder than I thought it would be. I tried to date right away, did not work and I backed off of that. We will get to him later. At least I had the presence of mind to see that putting a new man into the hole in my heart was not a healthy decision. I cried a lot, hurt and blamed Derek for all of it.

He immediately had a new girlfriend and is still with her. He resorted to partying, having lots of fun, spending tons of money and rarely seeing Caleb. Canceling visits and lying about what he was doing became a new habit. The list goes on. Do I think he is a horrible person? No, I do not. Quite the contrary. He had never treated us this way. He had intimacy issues, sure, but he was not "this guy."

I think he was behaving like a "normal" human being. He was hurting too, and was afraid of counseling. He hates to

Chapter Ten

open up, always has. I thought I could save him. We will address that poor pattern next chapter. He was merely lashing out in his hurt and anger, perfectly "normal." Not healthy, but typical.

light bulb

Here he is, behaving like a typical human being, and it made me angry. I was hurt he moved on so quickly. Then, I had a wake-up call in the state-required parenting class during a movie.

I did not want Caleb to end up like the children in those classroom movies. I cried so hard I had to leave. It was eye opening, big-time. I decided I should do everything to save our marriage and I tried to talk to Derek, but he was determined to get a divorce and be done with it. Easy. Clean. Done. No emotion. Sounds good. Only, that is impossible and everyone knows it.

He finally came over one night to see Caleb. We talked and he would not listen to me. He was telling me to let it go, move on. Throw away 7 years without a fight. I could not do it, did not want to. I was becoming angrier and angrier as I felt him robbing me of my chance to work. I felt he took my choice away and I felt powerless. Did Derek rob me of my choice to work? No. I *gave* my choice away.

He was about to leave and did not take Caleb with him; he merely wanted to stop by. Well, *I* thought he should have spent more time with him. I said this: "Caleb, your daddy does not even love you. He loves his job, golf and parties more than he loves you."

Yes. That is what I told my little boy; he was sad and began to cry. I told him his daddy did not love him. Derek was outraged, left and did not speak to me for days. I had fallen into a trap I did not think I was capable of falling into. I allowed my emotions to hurt Caleb unnecessarily and Derek was hurt, too. I was lashing out. I was in pain and I reacted. I did not make a wise choice.

Reacting is much easier, it requires no thinking. You never have to be the bigger person but, man, what I told my child was inexcusable. I sat with what I had done, all night. I became the mother portrayed in those classroom movies. I put my child in the middle of my emotions toward Derek. Not good.

I cried knowing what I had done was wrong. I picked up a book on divorce and began to read. The author was talking about how we should always show love for the other parent in front of the child—no matter what they do to you. You must be the bigger person. Unless the other parent is dangerous, there was no excuse for what I had done. He was reaffirming what I already knew.

Chapter Ten

Caleb had a right to know and love his dad with my full support.

Well, I forgave myself and made a choice right then and there. Do you hear me? I had to make a choice——a choice to never do it again. I wrote it down. I looked at it and then said it out loud. I can honestly say it has been about one year, and I have never done anything like that again. Not that I have been perfect, but I think before I act now.

Has it been easy? Oh no, very difficult, in fact. I could not simply make a choice that one day. The next time I was faced with something Derek pulled on us, I had to make the choice again. To the point where it has become a daily choice and habit. Now, I do not have to think about it and a new pattern is being created. I know saying something bad about him in front of Caleb would be harmful to his development. Anything he says, I just chalk it up to him dealing with this as he needs to, for a while. Seriously, I know that is what it is. He may choose to remain this way for the next 18 years, his choice, but I will not be sucked in. And by the way, I do not believe he will. He is healing too.

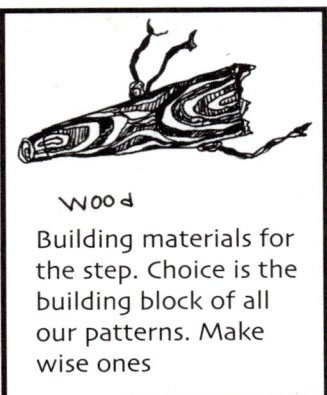

Building materials for the step. Choice is the building block of all our patterns. Make wise ones

Can I say he has given me the same courtesy of not talking negatively about me? No, I cannot, but that is not the point. Being a conscious person means you have to be the bigger person in most cases. If I want to keep living my life asleep, then I will react to his hate and it will become an endless circle of hurt for Caleb, and for me. **Have you experienced those days when you are eaten up with bitterness and anger?** Days you want to lash out, call the attorney and make him/her suffer? I have. What a waste of my day, my time and my energy. I make a choice *not* to call the attorney. I am not perfect, though. I get very close.

NEGATIVE THOUGHTS AND REACTIONS WASTE OUR PRECIOUS TIME.

Remember we were talking about the toilet and my grandpa? I told you I realized what I was doing when I allowed negativity to creep in. Remember I said I was missing something? Well, I have to say, even though I did not speak ill of Derek in front of Caleb, I was allowing myself to think negatively of him, and it consumed me. Day and night I thought about what he was doing to us by leaving. How could he not work on us? Leave the family? Let Caleb cry at night and have nightmares? **Why wouldn't he change?** What was his problem? Well, thinking like this is a waste of energy—a big one. I had another wake-up call.

Chapter Ten

One night, I get Caleb loaded up in the truck and we order takeout. We drive on the beach and I decide we will eat our dinner as the sun sets. Have you ever seen kite surfers? They are amazing and Caleb loves to watch. These guys get into the water on "wakeboards" and strap a huge kite to their torso. The wind propels them along the water and when so many of them get together, it is a sight to see. They do flips over the waves. It is incredibly cool! Caleb pokes his head out of the sunroof and laughs. He is so happy. He sits down and begins eating his broccoli.

"Mommy, I am going to get big and strong and learn to fly a kite like that. I will eat my broccoli and get bigger right now. I want a blue one when I am big. Will I be bigger tomorrow?"

He ate every piece of broccoli. We should eat on the beach more often.

Well, that was cute, but I cried. How is Derek missing this? His son wants to get bigger, he is finally really talking now and telling me his passions. He is becoming a little man. How could Derek miss this? He is out at a party and his son would love to watch him fly those kites. Derek used to fly them. He no longer does. Work is his life now, just as it was to my grandfather. Do I see a pattern? What is he thinking? Poor Derek. Poor Caleb. Oh, the tragedy...and then I woke up.

light bulb

What the heck was I doing? Caleb and I were having this great little experience eating on the beach, loving each other's company, laughing. Why did I spoil it by crying? Caleb did not want me to cry. Wait a minute... Sure, maybe Derek was missing it, but now I was, too. I allowed myself to go to that place of negativity and reacting again. By crying, I was missing Caleb's smile. I wasn't enjoying the *now*.

Hey, Sarah, wake up. You are not missing this! Caleb is here with you, teaching you, loving you. Enjoy this. Do not let negativity ruin your time with him. Stop it right now! I mean now! Jeez, God. Okay, I get it. I am awake.

I began to think of all the times I cried when I could have been enjoying him; all the times I thought about what Derek was missing and giving up. What a waste. I was not giving anything up. I was not missing anything. I still had a wonderful life with my son, and it was time to stop my negative behavior. Did I struggle with this one even after this day? Oh yeah. We all do. Again. CHOICE.

Every time those thoughts creep up, I have to stop and say, NO! It is not worth it. It feeds the bitterness... unhappiness... anger... stress... worry... fear. Positive thoughts are the antidote to all these words. I do not choose to miss out on the wonderful experience of watching my son grow up and we all know these years go by so quickly. I began to learn how to simply *be* in the moment.

Chapter Ten

A WORD UNSAID SOON FALLS DEAD. A WORD SAID, BECOMES ALIVE!

Have you been through a divorce and woken up years later? Did you miss those sweet years due to anger? Were you distracted by negative thoughts and behaviors? It is not too late to change, you know. You could make a choice and speak aloud your new, positive thoughts, after you have written them down. It is okay to talk to yourself out loud; I do it all the time. Allow me to explain the process.

First, I write all the negative thoughts on paper and find the positive lesson. I cross through the negative words and insert the new ones. I then take it one step further. I literally say out loud,

Pen and Paper
To create our own blueprint to the path to our purpose

"I am not missing a thing. I love my life. I love Caleb and we are happy. I am a strong person with a new and exciting life. My life is begining and I embrace the future. We are great. I love Derek. I wish him love and peace. He will be shown nothing but love and respect. He is a good man and anything he is doing right now, he is doing out of hurt."

Can you picture in your mind what that paragraph looked like *before* I changed it? I believe the word "hate" was previously in the text, also the word "fear." From here on out, *fear* is the new F-word. Deal? I do not want you cursing young lady, young man.

Do you see the pattern I was now developing? Writing it down. Seeing it on paper. Saying it out loud just as I did with the patch and the scars. The more you say it, the more it becomes truth. It works the opposite way also. If you write hate, anger and bitterness, and say it often, it becomes truth.

Do you send hate e-mails to your ex? Text messages? Hey, I did too. That seemed to be a constant struggle. You are not alone. Trust me, I understand, but there comes a time when we must make the choice to stop.

"George, this all sounds like some New Age, positive thinking, mumbo jumbo," you say with hesitation.

I know it does, but the countless books out there on positive thinking, work. Maybe you have not given them a chance because you did not use your crowbar; maybe you simply did not quite understand them. Some of them are what I call "college level of positive thinking." Trust me, there were many books I did not absorb because I had not laid any groundwork for the process they were preaching.

Chapter Ten

Maybe what you need is a book for "first grade level of positive thinking." We all need to start somewhere and I for one like to speak in layman's terms, remember? I am a simple person. I hope I am making it simple for you.

"Hey, do not forget your crowbar! I never let mine out of my sight!" I exclaim as George runs off to grab a pen and his journal. And when I say simple, it is not meant to insult anyone. I simply believe, the simpler, the better. We have it backward. I knew more in the first grade than I do now!

Please, guys, let's stick together and formulate a game plan. Let's see how building healthy, positive patterns can change lives. Looking at the lessons in each dark corner of our lives and connecting them, cause us to see our reason for being on this earth. Can you now see how I am finding my purpose for being alive, by changing my attitude and pulling out my magnifying glass? Don't you think it could work for you? We are getting closer, aren't we? How patient you are. You too, George.

So, you, yeah you. You have done it, haven't you? You have been like me, haven't you? Okay. So do it. Write it down. Say it out loud. Right now, say this.

"I make a choice. I will honor my child's father/mother in front of my child and others, at all times. My child has a right to love his father/mother with my full support. The

> *negative words stop here and now. I love my ex and I will show my ex respect, whether he/she does or not. I will not allow myself to waste one more minute on negative thoughts. I will not get sucked into the 'tit for tat' trap. I will quit missing days, months, years of being 'here' with my child, due to unhealthy reactions. I will begin showing my child how to create positive patterns and I will lead by example. Starting this very second, I make this choice."*

Hard to say? Yeah, I know. Just keep saying it. To the teens: If your parents are divorced, start by making the choice to become an example to them. You are never too young to begin changing.

Thoughts become words.
Words become actions.
Actions become habits.
Habits create patterns.

Are you starting to see why positive thinking isn't just a bunch of mumbo jumbo? Don't you see why I made it a DRILL? Drill all of this into your head, my friends. Positive thinking is the drill for each pattern. Drill those positive thoughts into every step. **It begins with one thought and one thought will change your life.**

"You know what, George, she has a very good point. I am starting to like her," you are saying with surprise.

Chapter Ten

Hey, I am glad you are coming around. You and about four people like me now. This is great. Let's start a club.

"I said , *starting to.*"

Oh. Sorry. There I go with my positive thinking again.

I bring this to light right here in the book because I want you to see I was now making choices. I did not randomly go out there and throw darts, and fffmmmuuummmp … well, the dart says … um, this is the reaction I will have. Now that I am learning how to become conscious and to make my own choices, well, I do not throw darts anymore. DARTS. Where was that lesson? Do not throw darts. Where did I learn about a dart? Oh, I remember. The eye doctor!

When I was two and the doctor put that patch on my eye, he told me something else. He said I also had to protect my good eye. I mean, hey, I only had one of those. I was instructed to wear goggles when playing sports as I aged. I was even told I was not to throw darts, ever, for any reason. Dangit, there goes my chance to be an Olympic gold medalist in dart throwing. Dangit! Wow. He did not want me to get hurt. He didn't know how right he was.

safety goggles

Protects our precious sight

light bulb

You know what, I like that. Don't throw darts—for your protection. Do you see the lesson in that? He was trying to hand me a tool and he did not even realize it. CHOICE. Stop throwing darts out there when you are deciding what to do in any situation. If you throw darts, you could injure yourself…like with alcohol, or have a stroke or give yourself cystic acne. You could poke your eye out when you were born with two good ones. Are you seeing how this all comes together? I certainly am. **So, quit REACTING to everything and everyone. Wake up!**

"Oh, sorry, George. Were you taking a nap? Man, everyone around me seems to be doing that!" I sigh.

Here is the secret to this book. I have shown you how I was taking everything "bad" or "challenging" that has happened to me, and made a choice to see the lesson in writing. By doing that simple task…the bitterness, fear, anger, depression, worry, guilt…all of it evaporated. Because by seeing the lesson and finding the pattern, I can easily see how nothing happened by accident. Everything that happened actually did happen for a reason, a wonderful one.

We say, **"Everything happens for a reason."** Do you really believe it? Do you realize what you are even saying? If you do not see the reason within days, do you forget to ask "why" months later? Years later? Do you just chalk it up to: "Well, only

light bu

Chapter Ten

God knows?" Maybe He is trying to tell you and you are not listening! Or maybe this awful thing in your life that "seems" to keep "happening" is not really an accident. **Maybe you keep repeating the same patterns**, and that is why it keeps happening! Have you thought about that? Maybe it will keep happening until you choose to see the lesson and make changes. In fact, I'm telling you it will!

You do not want to look, do you? Cause then, you might have to change and we do not like change. Change requires work. We have already established we like the easy fix. Are you the person who keeps saying, **"Why do all these bad things keep happening to me? WHY oh WHY? Poor me!"** Good question.

Why?

When I chose to see the absolute positive side of each dark moment—even if it took years—I began to love the fact it happened. Seriously. I am thankful for each time I hurt. Remember the cold dip? The pain really does make me strong. Bring it on, I say now! Bring it on. No pain, no gain.

EVEN IN DIVORCE, YOU CAN BE A SUCCESS

Yet, here I am still kind of feeling like a failure. I still do not like to fail, even after all these years. It took much work to eventually erase that word, huh?

I was trying to find a way to turn the following sentence around with my drill—— "I hate my divorce." One day, I am talking about Derek and myself, and how we have been helping Caleb through all of this to a friend.

My friend says, "Man, I wish we could have been like that. You guys are really an example to all of us. You should teach a class to people about how to handle the divorce."

I was floored. My divorce should be an example? I know we have not been perfect. Really? My failure could be an example and help others? Positive drill. Why not?

I examined our divorce with my magnifying glass and look at what I found.

Caleb was given love by both of us, equally.

Derek had begun to see Caleb more often. I met his girlfriend and gave her a hug. She gave me one, too. We even wrote each other a nice letter and practiced yoga in the same room.

Success!

Caleb saw that exchange of love.

We baked Daddy a cake on his birthday and

Success!

Success!

Chapter Ten

made him Father's Day presents.

Caleb quit having so many nightmares and the abandonment issues have disappeared.

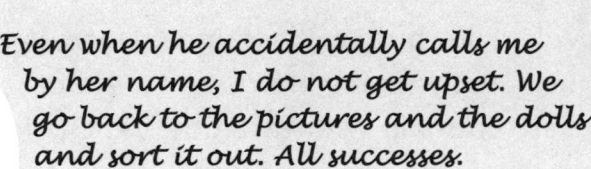

He becomes confused about the girlfriend and I have learned how to make him understand these changes in his own three-year-old language. Play therapy, it is called.

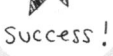

He understands now, really does like her and he feels safe to tell me about her.

Even when he accidentally calls me by her name, I do not get upset. We go back to the pictures and the dolls and sort it out. All successes.

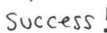

When Derek comes to pick him up, he is hugged by all of us. If I have friends over, they shake his hand.

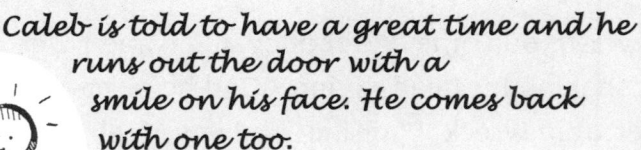

Caleb is told to have a great time and he runs out the door with a smile on his face. He comes back with one too.

If he ever says, "Daddy doesn't love me. He is always at work. I don't want to go over there today"—and he does still say that—I say, "Oh yes he does, Caleb. He has just been working hard for you. He loves you and cannot wait to see you. Now, I know you have fun over there and you know it. You have a really cool room at Daddy's house, with lots of toys. You go and get ready. He will be here in an hour. Let's set the timer, hide, and scare him like you love to do."

He smiles and goes under his tent to wait for his dad. Derek bought a wonderful new house with a special room for Caleb. He brags about it every time he comes home. I am genuinely happy for them.

We did not hire two attorneys. Nope. We mediated with my life coach for about $250. We were both fair with each other, then hired one attorney and had her do it all legally for us. The attorney told me only about one in every thirty cases is uncontested as ours was. That is only about 1% and is a huge success.

We did not waste our time and money and some judge out there is not shaking his head saying, "God help them. There goes another train wreck. Poor kids. I always feel bad for the kids." Nope, we are not one of those. Hopefully we never will be. Go, us! Thank you, Derek. You and I are still a team, like it or not.

Chapter Ten

"Woah! Look at all the success ribbons, George," you exclaim.

I am glad you noticed. I counted 13. Who says it is an unlucky number? I personally love 13.

Maybe you say, "Aw, man, we didn't do all that. We argue in front of our child. We cannot even do the child handoffs and require a third party to do them for us. Actually, the judge made us do it this way. He was mad at us for always being in court with our petty problems. When my child says his daddy doesn't love him, I say, 'You're right. He is a loser and you shouldn't like his new girlfriend either. She takes his time away from you. I don't like her and I bet she is no fun. You like me more, right? Please tell me she isn't more fun than I am, or I will feel threatened and become angry.'" Sound familiar to any of you?

Relax, that is normal. We have those thoughts because we are human, yet it is never too late. Sounds like you may need to take out a pen and begin writing that positive mumbo jumbo. Begin talking to yourself again. It works.

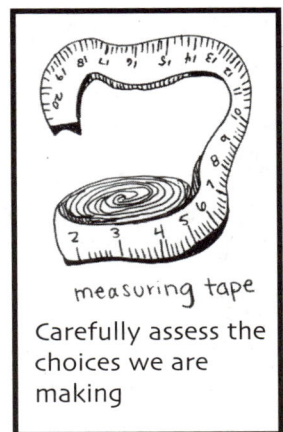

measuring tape
Carefully assess the choices we are making

Go ahead, don't believe me. Do not try it and you will keep having the paragraph back there happen to you day after day——year after year——until your child is grown and you both cannot even attend his wedding without drama, because you let it go too far. Go ahead, ruin his day. Create an unhealthy pattern for him. Maybe he will see it, and end up in a divorce court and put his kid in the middle, and the circle will continue. I would rather talk to myself and have people think I am crazy. What about you?

I want to talk to those of you who do have an ex-spouse who is "unfit." I realize many of you will not have a situation like mine. If your child is constantly resisting the visit with the ex, and you are not fueling the behavior, please take a closer look. There may be something seriously wrong. I am talking about my life in this book and as of this moment, I am unaware of any serious harm that could be brought to Caleb. Trust me, I am not a pushover merely because I am conscious. When I feel the best interest of my son is not put forth, I become the same mother lion you all do. If I ever feel as if he is in danger, I will take action. Please know I am speaking to those who are dealing with the daily pettiness eating away at our lives. You know who you are.

All of this is so simple. It is not rocket science and it has been said 100 different ways. Milleniums have passed since the first person discovered the process. I am not saying one

Chapter Ten

thing new. You may read this book and do nothing in your life. You do not have to. You can have a few laughs and say, "Good for her." But I am just hoping my book will allow you to see a regular person——someone who does not have a degree or fame or a life threatening disease that altered her life——a regular, run-of-the-mill girl changed her life and is happy.

I found my purpose and I am not in fear of doing what I need to do, what I was designed to do——full force. I love me, just as I am.

To me, this makes me as successful as anyone in the world, more than some actually. I am fulfilled. I am not empty inside. I find joy in merely living, just being. Some people never have one day in their life where they find purpose. They do not find fulfillment. They are empty. So, to me, I am a wild success, a grateful, humble one. You can do it too. We will connect all of this and make it easy. Deal?

Success!

We have more to learn here about old Derek, but first I want to say, we were the best of friends in our marriage. I was married to him for six years and have known him for over seven. I sum up why it ended. We wanted different lives. He loves his work and is outrageously successful. I am proud of him for that, but I loved people and a simpler life. We did not complement each other's life passions and were not partners as my parents and grandparents were. I also think I talk too much for quiet, Derek. He does not really like to share and my life is an open book, literally. I made a poor choice to marry a man with whom I did not see eye to eye. My choice and I have to live with the decision.

I did finally let go of my ego and say, "It is time to end this. Salvage what we can for a friendship." That was difficult because to look at myself again and say I have been through two divorces, well, that was pretty much the hardest thing I have ever done. He and I are working together now and I need you to understand something...

I shared what we have been through, to show we are not perfect. Also, notice it does get easier. If you are going through a divorce right now, you can let it all go. You will not wake up in pain forever and the bitter feelings will subside if you allow them. The work is worth the trouble, take it from us.

We continue to work daily and he is respected as a part of my life. I told you, I allow myself to love him and my son is the better for it. I read a book that calls this attitude "re-marrying your ex in divorce." So, many ask, "How DO you let it go?" Simple. Connect. Embrace your ex as he/she is *now* and simply let go. Easier said than done, but, you can do it!

Chapter Ten

Derek, you are a success in this as much as I am. You should be proud.

"George, give him a success ribbon!"

We will talk more about what I have learned and what patterns I clearly see need to be broken. It has only been one year since we separated, and we are now officially divorced. One year is not very long, however, that does not mean I lack insight into what our country faces with divorce and children in those divorces. I am sure I have told a few stories and you are thinking, "Hey, that happens to me every week." Yup, I relate. Let's get to talking and to changing. Change with me.

Let's give our kids a chance, shall we?

You need to get the sledgehammer out. We are finally going to use it.

sledgehammer

Are you excited, George?

tool time with tessie

Did you receive the message? Even in a failure, you can be a success. It can seem tough to do the work at first, but once you begin, it is the easiest route to take. I thank Derek right here and now for making my life drama free. I see many broken families live day after day with "drama."

Are you ready to do a little bit of work, too?

Take a look at the tools we found. In a dark moment, a "failure," we found an essential building block to any step. Wood!

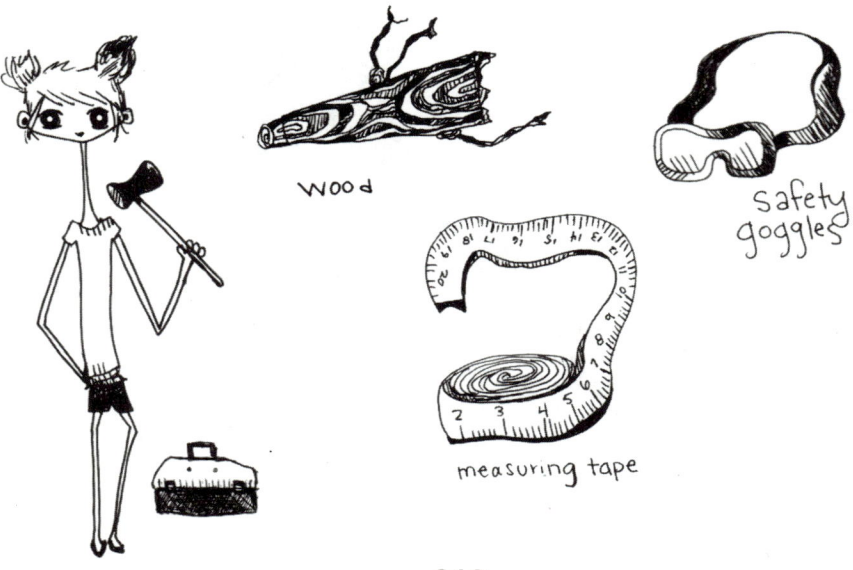

That brings me to my screw:

 **I AM GRATEFUL FOR THE DARK CORNERS OF MY LIFE**

I say what I mean and I mean what I say. Say it out loud with Tessie.

If you cannot speak these words yet, I suggest you grab your journal. You know what to do...

Be Conscious. Change.

STOP! Hammer Time

Breaking an unhealthy pattern is not only fun, it is liberating.

I have a black Labrador named Bogey. He is the most gentle, sweet-natured dog in the world—truly. He is well behaved, but one day he wandered over to the neighbors' yard and pooped there. Bill was not very happy. He and his wife are an elderly couple and they wave to me on occasion. I do not know them. My neighborhood is not one of those where people speak to each other, most keep to themselves. That is just how it is.

Bill made a copy of the homeowner's association agreement, highlighted the appropriate areas about the dog and left the document in my mailbox. Well, people have different reactions to different situations. Now, I could become angry about this action and start a war, unnecessarily, with my neighbor OR I could NOT start a war and realize he likes to work in his garden. He does not appreciate my dog leaving a mess in his yard, maybe he stepped in it. Bill does not have a dog.

I thought about this and I felt bad. Our yards have no fences and Bogey weighs 100 lbs. I cannot keep him on a leash because he needs to run. He ran through the "invisible fence" once—too smart for his own good.

Taking responsibility for Bogey was a choice and I made Bogey write Bill a letter. He said he was sorry, and we left Bill a bottle of wine and a Christmas card. Bogey signed it with his paw print and everything. Bill still did not wave at

Chapter Eleven

me at first, but at least I felt better. I try, every time Bogey goes out, to watch him more closely and make sure he does not wander over there. I really do feel bad; Bogey did too. He really wanted to write that letter.

Well, when Derek and I separated, it got worse. Not for Bill, for me. Taking care of Bogey and Caleb, and trying to figure out my new life was overwhelming. On top of it all, my dad was ill and I was stressed. I mean, letting Bogey out meant I did not always have time to see exactly where he went. My other neighbor realized what had happened between Derek and me, and I think they felt bad for us. They did not like the fact Derek moved out and would not even think of returning. They did not want me to be a single mom. See, when you are older and wiser, all of this divorce stuff seems silly. They told Bill and his wife what happened.

Trash pickup day is Monday and I have two huge cans and a recycle bin. I have to bring it all out there, keep Bogey under control, and make sure my three-year-old does not run into the street. I have to bring it all back in at night. Same scenario. **That simple task had become an overwhelming chore. Single motherhood had settled in.** Can you relate?

But, one day, I began to notice when I came home, the cans were up by the house, every Monday. I assumed the trash man did it for a while. I was too stressed to care. But one day I got to thinking and I knew it could not be the trash man and I waited by the window to see who did it. I am sure you can guess. It was Bill.

I stood there and cried. He is elderly and he rarely speaks to me but here he was, pulling up my trash cans. He never said one word about it. I used my "lunch break" and **decided I would never be too stressed or busy again to look at the little things in my life.** Live in the now, remember?

I wrote him a thank-you, and left him another bottle of wine. His wife called to thank me but she said Bill did not appreciate all the fuss. He had heard what happened and he did not like young ladies taking out their trash. It was a man's job, so he decided to do it for me.

That reminded me of my grandpa and I cried. How thoughtful and sweet. Someone I did not even know was trying to do his part to make sure a single mom was taken care of and show love. That meant much to me and I will not ever forget his kindness. Thank you, Bill. You kick off my week with a smile.

I continue to write him thank-you notes, cannot be helped. I am just so grateful. He waves to me now and we have finally spoken. I think he is a wonderful man; I adore him. Bogey may even poop in his yard when I am not looking, but I cannot be sure. If he does, Bill does not scold me.

Chapter Eleven

What if I had behaved like a brat and responded with negativity to his HOA letter? He never would have shown me that act of love and kindness. I would have missed out on my Monday afternoon smiles. I certainly would have missed out on our conversation the other day about God and philosophy. He is a retired school administrator and a wise, delightful person. One negative thought, one negative action would have changed everything and created a new poor pattern for Bill and me. I am so glad we are friends. Thank you, Bill. Again and again.

I began to think. What if I am missing something I could be learning about my marriages to Derek and David? If that one action changed everything with Bill, well, maybe I did not always react the way I should have with them. Maybe these divorces were more my fault than I think. Yuck. I do not want to pull out the magnifying glass on myself again. They are two different kinds of men. No. They were in the wrong and I can go on guilt free. It was not my fault.

Fine, I will look… and you guessed it, I finally saw the pattern.

They were not alike in the respect that David had a temper and Derek did not, but, oh the similarities. I do not want to go into much detail, to protect them both, but let's look at some general similarities. Then we will look at why I felt the need to marry men like this. Turns out, I thought I could save them, help them. Remember I told you that earlier? That is borderline codependency. Let us begin with the patterns.

Hey, we can use Spanish for our system, in honor of my dad.

¡UNO!

David was obsessed with his career. He was successful with money. He was an engineer and he embodied it heart and soul. Job was always number one. Family was clearly second and so was I. The perfectionism required in his job carried over into the home, big-time. His friends were mainly co-workers. No boundaries were set between work and home.

Derek was also obsessed with his career. He was successful with money. He is a land developer and he embodied it heart and soul. Job was always number one. Family was clearly second and so were Caleb and I. The partying and socializing required in his job carried over into the household. He traveled so much, we became second on his list of things to do. His friends were mainly co-workers. No boundaries were set between work and home.

light bulb

Not a healthy pattern.

Chapter Eleven

¡DOS!

David was not very close, in terms of relationship, to his immediate family. In fact, his father said these exact words to me at our first meeting: "Why are you dating David? He is such an @$$hole." Nice, Dad. Sounds like you guys are close. Because he was not very close with his family, he never wanted to spend time with mine. He did not see the point and it became a chore. That means I did not get to, either. I grew apart from my family. The strength I found in them was being pulled from me. I rarely heard him say, "I love you," to any of them. Mine says it every time we speak.

Derek was not very close, in terms of relationship, to his immediate family. In fact, his mother said these words to me at our first meeting: "We are so glad to meet you. Derek hasn't been home to see me in two years." Nice, Derek. Sounds like you guys are close. Because he was not very close to his family, he did not see the importance of being very close to me or Caleb. An arm's-length relationship, with few emotions, was acceptable. So, spending time with my family was pretty much out of the question. That means I did not get to, either. I grew apart from my family. The strength I found in them was being pulled from me. I rarely heard him say, "I love you," to any of them. Mine says it even when we fight.

light bulb

Not a healthy pattern.

¡TRES!

David decided how things were going to be run. If I did not agree, he would always win. I paid the price in pain. We were expected to live his kind of life. God was not the center of the home. I caved to whatever David wanted, just to be easy. I made most of the compromises. He promised me things before marriage, and changed after the fact. I did not know God was going to be "x"d out. David seemed to only really like God after he met me. In fact, he only seemed to like a lot of things after he met me, said I made him a better man.

Derek decided how things were going to be run. If I did not agree, he would always win. In fact, he would do things without asking, and say these exact words: "It is better to get forgiveness than acceptance." That was his favorite statement. He brags about it. He did not hit, though. Instead, he would smile and use his sales abilities to win me over. Both routes are manipulative. Both take my identity and credibility and throw it in the toilet.

We were expected to live his kind of life. God was not the center of our home. I caved to whatever he wanted to make life easier and made most of the compromises. He promised things before marriage, and changed after the fact. I did not know God was going to be "x"d out. Derek seemed to only really like God after he met me. In fact, he will tell you he only liked a lot of things after he met me.

Chapter Eleven

Said I made him a better man. Said he always knew he would not be able to hold up his end of the bargain, and he didn't.

light bulb

Not a healthy pattern.

¡CUATRO!

David did not respect nor support my opportunities for a career. He would let me do my thing, but he always made it clear his career and who he was in it, was above mine.

Derek did not respect nor support my opportunities for a career once I decided to have one again. In fact, I was told my newfound passion for the health of others was not to be discussed in front of his "friends." Said it was annoying, even when his friends asked——or co-workers, should I say. He said my passion was unimportant, and never listened to me when I was ready to talk about it. I mean, I was excited. He even put his fingers over my lips and asked me to be quiet so he could watch TV. Oh, he allowed me do my thing, but he always made it very clear his career and who he was in it, was above mine.

light bulb

Not a very healthy pattern.

Okay. That is about all I can divulge without getting too detailed and betraying their own issues with themselves. Everything I said would be something they have said to other people and are not ashamed to let be known. These are not too intimate to be revealed. They seem so easy to see, don't they? But, hey, when I left David, I just chalked it all up to his abuse and let it go that way. I did not stop to see what else was there. So, when I met Derek, all I saw was he was not angry like that. He was not cruel. In fact, he is so emotionless, he was the anti-David. Explains my attraction, I felt safe.

Now let's look at those traits, those patterns I kept choosing—I now see I chose them in every man I dated—let's look at where I was dysfunctional.

¡UNO!

I allowed these men to obsess about their careers. In fact, I am so supportive, in a way, I feed it. They want to be successful, I support it. I did not help create healthy boundaries between work and family. I allowed myself to be second. Sure, I would say things now and then. But, in the end, there were never any consequences to these actions. When I finally put my foot down with Derek, he left for good.

Also, by not having friends outside the office, I was the only friend they had. They relied on me for everything else. This allowed little room for me to have a healthy life outside of my husband. Codependency, they call it. I felt I had to help

Chapter Eleven

them, save them. Give them strength. A savior complex, is one way of describing it. Isn't that actually just my EGO?
Not a healthy pattern.

¡DOS!

Both these men placed zero importance on being close with their own family, for various reasons. That is their choice, which does not mean I cannot have a relationship with a man who is not close with his family. Please note my grandmother did not tell my mom *I love you* and she was distant from her for years, yet she broke her patterns. My mother decided family was important and was going to do everything in her power to change things, and she did. She always accompanied my father to his family's home. He was encouraged to love them. She did not pull him away from them, his source of strength. A healthy family is a source of strength. It is not your sole source, but it is an important one.

Both my men chose not to break these patterns. They remained distant from theirs, they remained distant from mine, and therefore they remained distant from me. After all, I became their only family and I was second. What does that tell you? Their "only family" was second! I was weakened by not having my family's intimacy that had shaped me all those years.
Not a healthy pattern.

¡TRES!

When both men met me, they will tell you they made changes only *after* meeting me. They saw my joy and figured they needed it too. They decided to find God, not because they really wanted to, but for me. I think they initially wanted it, but having a spiritual life requires work and neither of them wanted to do that. Hey, I am not talking about religion here. I am talking about Spirit. I gave you permission to substitute the word GOD in the beginning of the book. Neither of them even wanted to listen to their inner voice. Had they practiced some sort of yoga or meditation, I would have been happy. No meditation. No prayer. They tried; went through the motions. Trust me, if they had some sort of connection to Spirit, I would not be writing these last few chapters.

Therefore, we had zero spiritual connection—none. I felt empty. My spirit is what drives me, drives a lot of people. Quit debating over who has the right words, people. Just be spiritual, I say. So, all the things they promised me went right out the window once we were married and we led superficial lives. I allowed it. Kept thinking I would show them God and felt as if it was my responsibility. More codependency. They sucked me dry. I gave them all I had and they could not feed my spirit. I let them plug into me and drain me, expecting nothing in return.

Not a healthy pattern.

light bulb

Chapter Eleven

¡CUATRO!

This was not about careers, it was about passions. Just so happens we all let our passions provide our careers. I wanted my mine to seem important. I wanted to be seen. I wanted my reason for being here to be acknowledged. Because neither one of them could give me that respect, I eventually lost respect for their careers, their passions. If this kept me second, well then, I no longer wanted to be supportive.

I was with Derek longer, and after six years of full support, I pulled the plug. He did not like that, so he ultimately chose his passion over me. Why wouldn't he? I had allowed myself to be number two all those years with no consequences. Why wouldn't he choose number one? I would have. I gave up ME for them. I let mine die just to help them, to save them.
Not a healthy pattern.

light bulb

"FFFWWWWEEEEWWWW," I say as I wipe my brow. That is that, about as articulate as I can possibly get. Two men…the same but different and this one time, different was not good. It was the SAME I should have been looking at. So, now that I have broken out the magnifying glass, examined the patterns I allowed, looked at myself and my "codependent nature", my "savior complex"—— my "ego."
 … **NOW what? Anyone? You? George? Anyone?**

SLEDGEHAMMER TIME!

IT'S HAMMER TIME!

Seriously, I cannot tell you how good this feels. Because I promise you—promise you—I decided to break it out while writing this very book and you are here with me. So, without further ado ...

Chapter Eleven

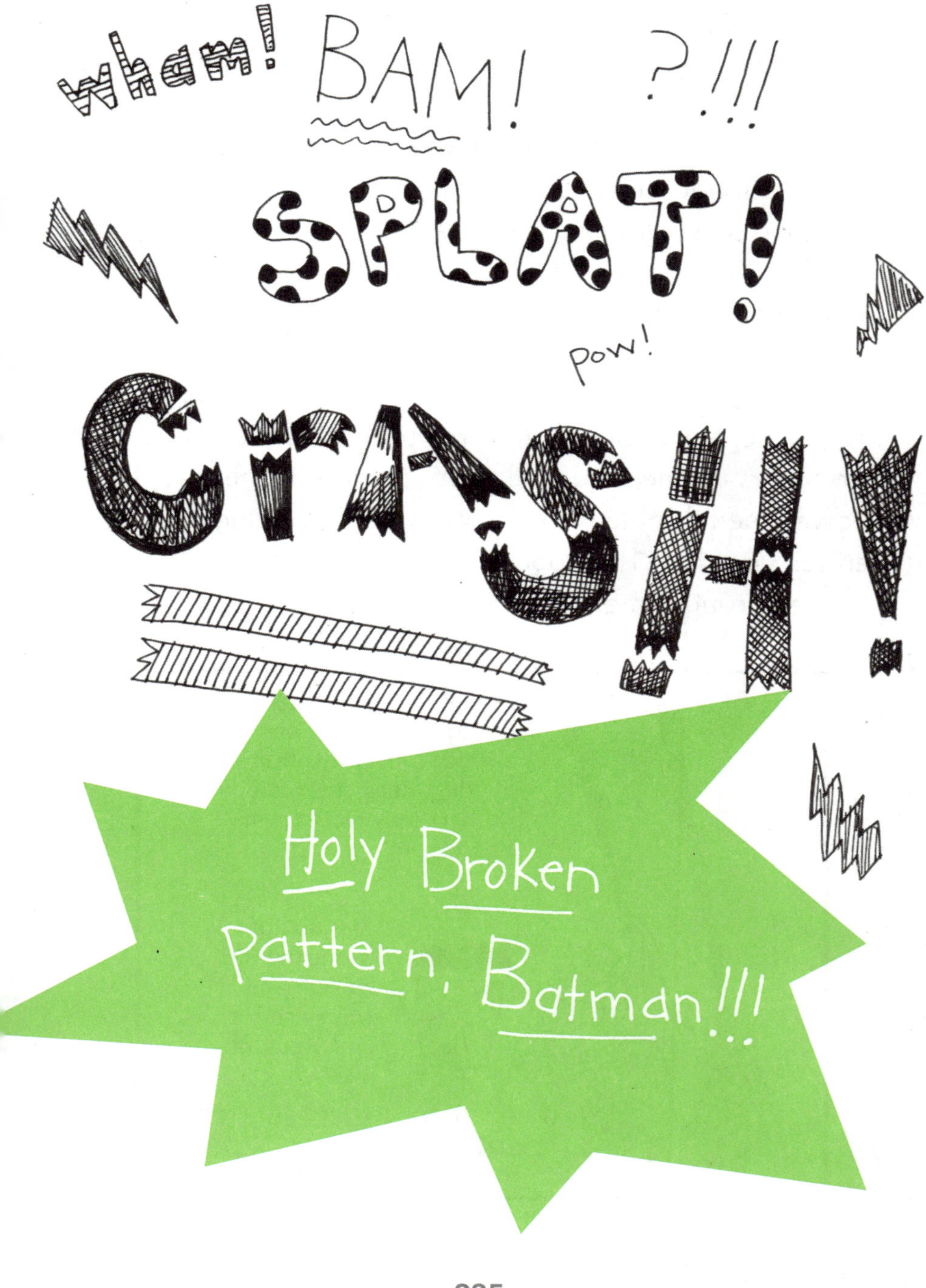
wham!
BAM!
?!!!
SPLAT!
pow!
CRASH!!
Holy Broken Pattern, Batman!!!

I am not lying as I write this, but I have tears in my eyes. **I just broke a pattern that has been with me since I was a little girl.** One that has caused me physical, mental and spiritual pain. **It feels so good and all my fear is gone.** I know I will not end up with the wrong type of man ever again. No one will take "me" away.

I have regained all my power. I gave the "flood" back to myself. I thought men were supposed to flood my dry spirit. How can someone who is draining you, flood you? Impossible. Never occurred to me to unplug the dam, about two blocks up the road, and allow them to come! I had allowed men to plug into me. Well, no more plugs for me, I can tell you that. The floods have come and I weep over the joy they brought me.

Sweep away negative thoughts and actions which prevent us from acting. Keep them handy; others may blow them back onto our path

We do not want the filth of fear and worry to rot our steps, do we?

broom   mop

Chapter Eleven

Do you hear me? I do not have fear anymore. None. No "F" word. I am not bitter toward these men. I love them. I thank them, they taught me. I do not regret my marriages to either one. I am not a failure! I love all of my life.

Wood Stain

Seal the pattern once it is set

So, take out the broom and mop, two tools we need. Sweep those "F" words off the new step once it is built. Once they are gone, seal it with belief. Go ahead, put a sealant on it. Do not allow the filth of fear to seep back in. NO MORE FEAR! What a release! NO MORE FAILURE!

I will not allow myself to say these words again: "I won't end up with the wrong man because I will never get married again. That will fix it. No one can harm me if I don't let anyone in." Have you ever said that? I did. Well, now, instead I say:

"I know I will not allow myself to end up with the wrong type of man again. Not because I won't let anyone in, I will just be more careful *who* I let in. Marriage is a wonderful, healthy institution if both parties are healthy. I see the red flags now. I will pay attention and change. Unhealthy patterns in every potential "mate" are now called red flags. I will not try to save anyone. I can't. It is impossible. They must save themselves. I don't need to be needed. I want to be WANTED!

> I will not give up "me" or my passions for someone else's, *no one* else's. I take my power back. I am no longer viewed through a man's eyes. I am now only viewed through my eye——my spiritual eye——my third eye. So, I do have two eyes. YES! The patch did make my eye see again! It did retrain my brain to tell my eye to see. It was a success. You simply did not notice, doctor, because you were looking at the wrong one. I have a third eye, didn't you know?"

Did you get that, George? **I do have two eyes, one that sees the world and one that see the lessons in the world.** Two eyes. Thank you, God, for my only one earthly eye. If I had two, maybe I would not have been forced to use the third one. I am blessed. I am thankful and I have come full circle with my eye, and the patch.

Did you notice that? Full circle. You still have your blindfold, right? I will help you understand you need to blindfold your two eyes in order to open your God-given third one. However you want to view it is fine with me. Third eye, spiritual eye, whatever you want to call it. It is there. We all have one. Maybe your brain just needs a little re-training. We will get there.

I also want to say something to Derek. Do I think I am better than he is? No, sir. I hope you have been able to see I wrote as much about me as I did him. I mean, having codependency issues is no fun, kinda stinks. He took

Chapter Eleven

advantage and I let him and so forth. That is the point. We were both unhealthy and we gravitated toward each other. I have made a choice to break my patterns and change.

He *is* changing some of his patterns. I see him spending a lot more time with his family. Great! His mom and sister are coming this weekend. That makes me smile. I hope they become closer. God bless all of them, and I wish them the best in life. I mean that. He now spends more time with Caleb *after* the divorce, than before. I beam with happiness for them both and encourage Derek to take him as often as he chooses. He is his father, after all—— and a good one at that. Hey, we are not perfect. We argue. We debate. But in the end, we both end up doing the right thing, for all our sakes.

Next, we are going to talk about my new man pattern. Remember I told you I tried to date and then quit? Well, a man named John came into my life and taught me a few things about myself and he is my friend. Notice I said "friend." Friendship is such a special gift and a strong foundation for any romantic relationship. Want to hear what he taught me?

"Do we have a choice?"

You know the answer to that one by now, George.

You always have a choice.

tool time with tessie

Whew! Did you see that? I figured out a way to self-diagnose my unhealthy patterns and correct them. Do you feel uncomfortable visiting a counselor? Do you feel you do not have the money to attend a session? I am not making promises, but I am showing you what I have done and am giving you tools to make changes. It is a start. Maybe by working a bit on your own, you will heal and let go. Can't hurt to try.

Let's applaud ourselves for using the sledgehammer. We also found our stain and mop and broom.

Tessie's screw for you is:

I TAKE MY POWER BACK WHEN I BREAK A POOR PATTERN!

Become empowered; it feels so good!

Do you need to write in order to free yourself from the pain? You can be your own best "counselor."

Be Empowered.
Act.

Lamp, not Spotlight

If you do not take life one step at a time,
you will become overwhelmed.

So, this guy. Are you curious? I met John in an interesting way. I was on the porch of a restaurant. It has amazing, healthy foods and I practically live there. I was just sitting there talking to someone about the property I purchased to build a wellness center. Told you I was doing that. We will get there.

This guy comes up to me and says, "Hey, I've been overhearing your conversation and I think I have a friend you would like to meet. His name is John. He owns a holistic clinic and maybe you two would have something to talk about. I believe he needs space to move his clinic. Here's his number."

I call John and we talk for 45 minutes. Allow me to tell you what he does. He owns a clinic with two partners. They treat lymphedema. In layman's terms, when your lymphatic system does not release fluid from your body properly, it needs to be manually drained. If a patient has had any portion of the lymphatic system removed due to cancer, let's say, the body needs to find a way to release the fluids.

John's clinic has a non-surgical procedure to reduce swelling, the Vodder method, for not only cancer patients, but others as well. The same method is encouraged for a maintenance program in healthy patients, as a means to eliminate toxins. I encourage you to try it. They helped my father when he had swelling due to congestive heart failure.

Chapter Twelve

So, we plan to meet to see my architectural plans. We hit it off right away as friends. His energy blew my sox off. I did not realize someone could be more passionate than I am. Do you know what one of the first things he ever said to me was? "I LOVE ME." Get that! **He loves himself just as he is.** I thought that was my line. I am always saying, "I love me." I was even called a "My Sexual" once because I

love me so much. Ya know, I should start a My Sexual Club. Wanna join? You gotta love yourself first though and prove it, very strict rules. Hey, get your mind out of the gutter. I mean love YOU, as a person. Jeez, people.

We agree to continue talking about the merger. During this time, I was separating and so was he. He was not married but he was ending a three-year relationship. No big deal. We were friends and didn't think too much of it. Once I was finally out, we went on a few dates, but it did not really work for either one of us. **I am healthy minded**, and we decided it was best to remain friends only. I am not saying it was an easy choice. There was an obvious attraction, but we both had work to do on ourselves and we did not want to do the "rebound thing"—— not worth it. I did not want to fall into the trap that seemed to snare so many.

We remained friends for seven months, hung out, worked through stuff and tried to heal. We kind of got out there and tested the waters of dating others. Not much happened. Trust me, the dating world was not very promising. I mostly had fun and explored a bit. John tested the waters, but admittedly swept his issues under the rug.

In this time, I was able to know him as a close friend. He is definitely the one everyone wants around when you want to have the best time you have ever had. Call him. He would have you out on the town in five minutes or less, guaranteed. Go ahead. Call him. He wants you to.

He has flaws and he will tell you. I am sure there are people in our small town happy to spill all his secrets. Trust me, he has imperfections, but I know no one like him. **He breaks all molds.** He does not live in anyone's box. No one puts John in a box. Go ahead and try. I dare you.

He taught me about music and introduced me to a band called Sigur Ros. They are Icelandic, and completely out of the mainstream. I fell in love with them and I have written this entire book listening to them only. They move me to tears and smiles, to emotions I have never felt before. In July of this year, they were performing in Spain and I wanted to go.

I text him, "Let's go to Madrid next week to see Sigur Ros."

Chapter Twelve

He texts, "I don't have a passport anymore."

I text, "So?"

You know me by now. I will go to Madrid within seven days, without a passport. We will just figure it out, right? Tap dance. So, we did. I found a way to get him a passport in three days.

He could not swing a lengthy time off work, and Derek had Caleb, so we had 48 hours in Madrid. I loved traveling with him. We are insane.

"Did I tell you he is as crazy as I am? Oh, I didn't? Well, maybe he is crazier, actually. George, let's just say he talks to leprechauns, okay? Guardrails don't have nothin' on this guy!"

We explored Madrid and uncovered every pebble. A 16-hour round-trip plane ride resulted in a mere 48 hours abroad. It was amazing. I cried the entire night out of sheer, overwhelming emotion. The music is powerful, let me tell you. **I deepened a spiritual connection with John.** I had never had one with a man before. I did not know what else to do but cry; it was so beautiful. I was rendered speechless for the first time in my life and he never let me forget it.

So, we decided to try and date. But you know, without going into all the details at this point, we were not ready. I mean, all those years with poor patterns in relationships … both of us … cannot be fixed in seven months. He was not a very good little boy, he will tell you that. He hurt me and I did not deserve the way he did it.

But, point is, he was not ready to be in a healthy relationship. He still has many patterns he needs to locate. He cannot even break them until he does. Remember? It is harder than it seems and he cannot do it without his magnifying glass. I just handed him one and he hasn't used it yet. He must make the choice. I am done saving my partners, remember? I will not concern myself with whether he does or not and it feels liberating.

PATTERN CHANGE!

Here is another lesson I learned, forgiveness. John had to come face me and apologize for the hurt he caused. Many people would have told him this: "Give me a few days and I will be over it. Let me think about what to do with you. **Maybe** I'll find it in my heart to forgive you."

Well, in the moment he asked for my forgiveness, I had a vision. I am always seeing things nowadays. You all know that by now. Anyway, I saw myself in front of God, prostrate and begging him to forgive me for things I do over and over. We all repeat these unhealthy behaviors

Chapter Twelve

again and again. Do we not?

I have to say, it would be absolutely heartbreaking if He said to me, in that moment of repentance, "Give me a few days and I will be over it. Let me think about what to do with you. *Maybe* I'll find it in my heart to forgive you." That would kill me.

So, I forgave him, and it is one of the first times in my life I have understood what unconditional love is——loving someone despite their mistakes, like the spelling test. He made an *F* in our relationship and friendship, but I saw him absolutely repent. There is a big difference in someone who repents and someone who says they are sorry to simply get out of a punishment. Trust me. I know when I am looking at the real deal, when I am using my third eye at least. And, even that is not for me to judge. I forgive——with no strings.

drill bit

Forgiveness
You must forgive to love

drill bit

Unconditional love
Treat others when they repent as you would want to be treated

Now, cool thing is, I wrote this book through all of this. I became strong, as I worked on myself. I found myself and the floods came—with God's help and tools—but I did do it and John did not do the work for me. **I do not feel fulfilled because I have a man.** In fact, just the opposite. I do not have a man and I am the happiest I have been in 12 years. Twelve years!

I am whole. I am flooded. I am happy. I am free and I am loving me. I have all my power back—all *without* a man. Go, me!

That is a record for me. I always have a man, always. It is the holiday season, I do not have one *and* I am still happy.

"What do you think about that, George? Is this a success?" I inquire.

"You bet!"

Some people never enjoy one holiday alone. They allow emptiness to consume them and think they need a partner to feel fulfilled. Hey, I understand. I did it for years but not anymore. This is a success. I am a success this

Success!

Chapter Twelve

year. Christmas 2006... I love it. Here is my point. Some believe once you obtain your goal, you will be happy. But you must be happy first. Your goal will simply come to you.

"George, this girl is something else. She kinda drives me crazy, but I am warming up to her," more of you are saying.

I am so glad. Looks like I am gaining more friends. Wanna meet John's leprachaun?

"Don't push it."

Touché.

We could have fallen into the trap of helping each other, crying on each other's shoulder, clinging to one another for fulfillment and I never would have maintained my power. That is why I spoke of him. He is the first one, in all the years of my man patterns, where I was healthy minded.

drill bit

Awareness
Keep your wits about you. We would not want to miss any "red flags", now would we?

I do need retraining on some old issues with boundaries. We should talk about them in a minute. Hey, I just got divorced. Having a boyfriend is not the same as having a husband and I am learning how to retrain my brain back to that concept. It takes time but I am doing it. I am fully aware of the problem and that is the key.

Also, there is Caleb. I know Derek has a serious girlfriend and I encourage him to be with her if she makes him happy. But after much counseling, I realized Caleb was not ready... not yet. He still has more work to do and I have more work to do with him. John was not quite ready for Caleb either and he was honest about it. It was difficult to tell me, but he eventually did. Maybe not in the way I had hoped, but he did do it.

Let me tell you, if you do not want a relationship with a single mom or dad, then don't. Be honest. It is not an insult. Before I had a child, I did not want to either, but I do want all of you to at least open your minds. Because sometimes we have this "box" of what we think we want, and we are afraid to see it another way. I, for one, am not putting myself in a box. I have no clue what kind of man is meant for me. Age. Kids or no kids. Divorced or never married. I do not know and do not want to know. Let me tell you something my mother taught me, and this is the first time it really hit home to me.

The Bible has a verse that says this: *Thy word is a lamp unto my feet and a light unto my path.* Now, you may not like the Bible. Okay. You don't have to, but listen to what it says.

Chapter Twelve

I happen to think the Bible is pretty cool if you read it correctly. I know I may sound sacrilegious to some of you, but I think Jesus is very cool. He has the coolest stories. Mine cannot compare. If I lived back then, I would have been His stalker. Yup. I would have stalked Jesus and I think He would have let me hang with him. He would not have minded I talk to things that are not there. I think He would have encouraged it. **I like talking about God to people. I keep Him real in my life and I know I will never change.** So, do not think I am sacrilegious. I don't think He would say so.

Anyway, it is saying God lights our path with a lamp. Did you hear me? A lamp. He did not say SPOTLIGHT. Think about it. If we see too far down the road, it can become overwhelming, can't it? We begin to worry. **Sometimes we worry about things that never happen.**

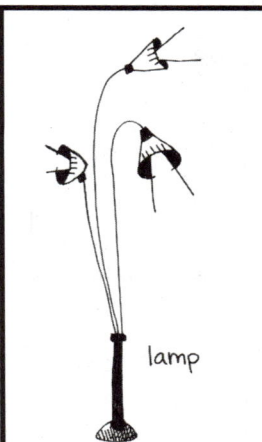

lamp

The lamp represents the light bulbs we are collecting. Screw them in one at a time. We do not want to become overwhelmed

I liken it to a forest. You do not really want to know all the scary things out there in the dark forest, do you? But if you have a mere flashlight, or lamp, then you can only see what is right in front of you, one step

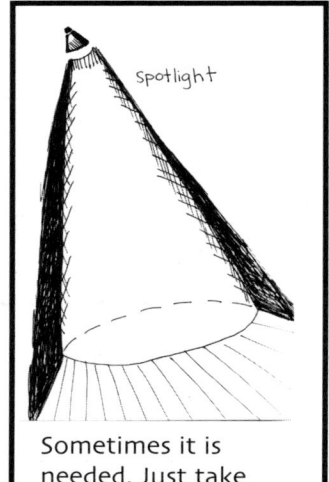

Sometimes it is needed. Just take care in how long you leave it on

at a time. Trust me, if you had a spotlight, you might see some things in that forest you really do not need to be seeing. It might freak you out. Do you see why we might be collecting light bulbs? Could they be so we can take it one little step at a time? We will get there.

I understand we need the spotlight for the bigger picture from time to time. It takes practice to know when to turn it off. I will be perfectly honest, there are people in my life I ask to turn it off for me. They see when I am becoming overwhelmed and they say the simple words, "Sarah...LAMP!" SWOOSH...and the light goes dim. I appreciate them so much. They help me remain in the moment.

What is my point? For the first time in my life, in the man department, I am in no rush. I do not want to know the outcome. John came into my life to teach me and test me and my broken patterns. He was there to aide me in finding my strength, and shine a lamp on patterns I was not seeing. Even in the darkest times the two of us shared this past year, I have learned and gained strength. He was used to shift me. Everyone needs that person.

Chapter Twelve

So, after a relationship ends and you meet the next person … be careful and make wise choices. You can either have a rebound or a shift partner, your choice. To have the shift partner, you must break out the sledgehammer though, or you just repeat the same ole pattern over and over. Hey, I made mistakes and I am learning. Point is, *this* time I am actually paying attention! It is a process, but it is getting easier. Trust me.

Do you know what else? I am writing this book, day and night. I do not want him to see all of this yet; I want it to be completed first. All he knows is I am writing a book that will help people. He knows no details. I have never written before, EVER. I am tap dancing again, and do you know what he says?

"Sass, I am so proud of you. *I think what you are doing is awesome. You are gonna do great things with this, I just know it."*

Did you hear that? He is proud of me and he has not read one page! Not one. He has not even met George yet! Or you! He thinks I will do great things. Notice, John "sees" me. He does not have to read it to know he is proud. He assumes if I wrote it, then it must show "me" in it. If you get to see "me" he thinks you will like me, because he likes me. If you like me, then you must like my book. He is proud no matter what I do. **Is that a pattern break?** Um … yeah, big-time.

Notice we are not plugged into each other. I like to put it like this: There is an imaginary ball of energy between us. We both feed the motion of that ball with our energy. **We gain strength from one another.** When one gives, the other gives back and the ball remains in motion. We both gain our power from the same source.

Have you ever been in someone's presence and fed off their energy? If it is positive energy, you feel high and energized when you leave their sight. If it is negative, you feel drained and low. Well, that is what I am saying. With my two husbands, I felt low and drained. With John, I felt high and energized.

If I am "alone" and do not have a fairy tale, happy ending to share yet, what is the point? I guess I could have waited until I was 80 years old to write this book. I mean, I only brought out the sledgehammer while writing this. Give me a break. I do not know how this is going to end. I am only 33. I have a lot more to learn.

I keep trying to tell you I am just like you, only a little different. **You wanna get out the sledgehammer?** Get it out. Use it and you will be right where I am, rebuilding a pattern. It is going to take time for it to become a habit and keep this pattern going. One step at a time though, right? Every time I am approached by a man, I have to remember to use my third eye and make a choice. If

Chapter Twelve

I see a red flag, GONE! No more chances. You are out! The tests will continue to come.

I can sit home every Friday and Saturday night if that is what it takes. I will not say yes, just to say yes. So many people tell me, "Oh, go out. Have fun. You can't sit home. Guys are asking you out. Go." Well, the right ones are not. If a right one does, I will say yes. Otherwise I will go out with girlfriends, guy friends or stay in with my cool lil boy or write.

CAUTION! CAUTION!

Place it around our step as we are re-building. We need to keep others with "red flags" out of our work area. caution tape

Yeah. Maybe I will write another book about how I went crazy in my house and somehow ended up owning 100 cats. Okay, kidding. I like dogs. And I'm using my lamp, remember? I don't need to see any further down the road at this moment.

Use this principle in all areas of your life; it applies to everything. Take it from former Miss Worry Wart, me. It does. We need to take the mop and broom to "worry" right now. Use this lesson and get them ready.

Goodbye, worry. Nice knowing you. You wasted enough of my time. See ya.

Now, what if I told you after all of that: John was unfaithful to me. Does that change any of my lessons? Any of my learning? No, it doesn't. Remember the cold dip? Feeling the pain made me stronger.

And I want to say something right here:

TRUST YOUR INTUITION!

I knew what was going on deep down and did not leave until I had proof. Why did I wait? The "F word" is the answer to that. Can any of you relate? It won't happen again, I can tell you that much.

Ya just know...ya just know.

Also, my sister, Alison, saw straight through John, just as she did with David. But this time, instead of becoming distant from one another, I actually kept an eye out for red flags and she and I are closer than ever. Not too difficult to break patterns once you locate them, eh?

THREE MEN——Abused, abandoned and betrayed. But look closer. I wrote a book, had a spiritual awakening, gained my power back and learned to love ME. Thank you, "men."

Chapter Twelve

I have learned from my experiences and I love all three of you.

I AM *ME* AGAIN!

For me, this was such a refreshing lesson and journey. I hope you felt a breath of fresh air after the last three chapters. I know I did and we do not have the end to the story, a cliffhanger. Just enjoy the dance. You never know when the music will change... enjoy the dance.

I am almost ready to tell you what we are going to do with the tools we acquired in our toolbox.

You are being incredibly patient, but first I want to tell you about a young lady I have been helping. We still need a few more tools. I need to get some of you off of this "Hollywood" image thing. Yes, you. The one who thinks you are not as good-looking as someone else, therefore, you are not very happy with your life. You want to change things about your physical body that should be left alone, like my scars.

Yup. We're gonna have a talk! We are going to let Lindy help us——a seventeen-year-old girl. We already referenced me and my scars, and I have a feeling they did not convince some of you. So be prepared, plastic surgeons, I am going to try and take away some of your business. I am not saying you do not have your place. I know you help some regain their confidence, but you know the ones who should not be in there and shame on you for cutting them up.

Chapter Twelve

Somehow I do not think my book is going to be in the waiting room of dermatologists and plastic surgeons everywhere.

tool time with tessie

Do you want to work? Do you know the real you? I hope I have inspired you to find him/her.

I really do love finding our tools.

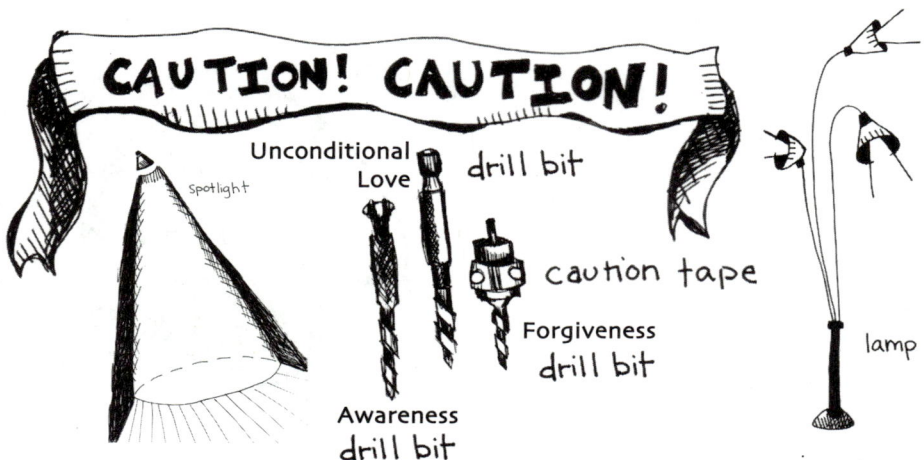

Let's all screw in our affirmation together:

I FEEL SAFE TO TRY AGAIN.

I must tell you, I was nervous to date again but I would not change the result. Thank you, John. I am dancing again.

Are you afraid to dance? Do you love others unconditionally? Have you learned how to forgive? Write. Connect your own dots and heal.

Be Passionate.Connect.

Botox Gives You Amnesia

Quit erasing your scars, your lines. You will forget the lesson they were supposed to teach you.

I lived in Jacksonville, Florida, and I remember the first year the NFL Jaguars came to town. I was about 24, I believe. It was very exciting and I happened to be a huge football fan. Alison and I, along with a couple of friends, decided to attend a Monday night football game against the Steelers. It was unreal. We splurged and bought tickets in row D on the 50-yard line. At our stadium, that means you are sitting in the exclusive, club level section. Here we were, just like the good ole tennis days with the best seats in the house. Tessie and Duffy, looking for yet another adventure.

I did notice things around me, though, now that I was older——things you do not notice as a child. Sometimes I wish I could go back to those days of being blind to the superficiality of this world. The people sitting in these seats were not very nice. They were talking down to the waiters and complaining about everything.

One woman was sitting behind me and, I promise you, she was wearing the same outfit Olivia Newton John wore in Grease. No, not the sweet one——the bad, black leather one in the last scene. I looked more like the "sweet one" with my blonde ponytail, polo shirt and white sneakers. She wore fake eyelashes, and black stilettos completed her ensemble. How could she even sit down, I wondered? That getup was so tight. I could not even imagine moving in it.

I am not one to judge people by their appearance, but I

Chapter Thirteen

thought, "What the heck?" This was the NFL, not a nightclub. I soon realized most women in there looked like her. Oh well, I thought, different is good. I was the one who looked different.

I decided not to give her another thought until she began to complain about us. We stood up as a big play was setting up, i.e. 3rd and 27. Everyone stands up during a play like that. Well, not the club section, apparently. She said these exact words, in her high-pitched, tiny voice: "Could you please sit down? I cannot see and you are only supposed to stand up when there is a touchdown." Huh? Was that the rule? I had been to numerous games and never heard it before.

I did look around, and sure enough, the club section was very quiet, refined, and sitting down as the rest of the stadium went nuts. It was a three-point game and there were two minutes left on the clock. If the Steelers did not make this third down, we would most likely win. Stand up, you snooty club people. I decided right then and there, I never wanted club seats again. I simply could not have fun.

Well, they did not stand up with us and she kept complaining. She told a waiter on us and we got into trouble. I called her out on it, but we had to sit down. Funny thing was, a big recording artist was sitting right behind her and I did not notice him. I am just not like that; I was there for the game.

Well, he liked me and my friends and the fact we were rebels in the club zone. We were invited by his bodyguards to attend a private function after the game. I will not tell you who it was, but he is famous. You all know him. I do have to admit we knew we would be the only white girls there. We looked so homegrown, young and innocent. Ponytails. Shorts. Polo shirts. Sneakers. We were excited and the guard told us the secret location. We followed his limo there. Let the night begin.

Many of the Jaguar players were there as well. I was working in the apartment industry and many of them happened to live at my property. They do that when they first move to town—rent apartments. Never know if you are going to get cut, right? It was nice to see familiar faces and we immediately felt at home. Only white girls, but Ali and I were used to that. Mexico, remember? Anyway, it is not about race; we so obviously did not fit in, but we had a blast. To us, different was always good. My sister and I did not drink, never had and we did not start that night. Again, we were the ONLY ones doing that as well. We didn't care. We laughed and had so much fun with these people. There were girls everywhere, all dressed up, dying to talk to them, and we had their full attention.

I looked over to see my sister trying a cigar, with the recording artist. He thought she was hysterical. The cigar smoking did not really suit her, but everyone around just

Chapter Thirteen

loved her and her big personality. We were staying true to who we were.

One of the football players told me, **"You always seem to have fun, without drugs and drinking. I envy you. We all do. You are just so real, Sarah. I love talking with you."**

I relish a compliment like that. I enjoyed talking to him as well and told him so. We talked all night and became friends. He lived in the apartments and I loved hanging out with him—just friends. I was sad when he was transferred to the Packers. He was a good guy. They all were.

Now, what is my point here? Did you hear what he said? All of these people were millionaires. They were famous. Trust me, you know them as household names. I made like $35k per year, lived in an apartment and drove a Mazda. We obviously stuck out like sore thumbs for many reasons. But he said they envied ME, because I was ME and I was happy like that.

Do you see the success in that, people? Even famous music stars and sports heroes long to have confidence to just be themselves and here I was, loving me just as I am. That was a huge success for me. Some people never have one day in their life where they do not feel as if they must conform to have a good time.

We ended up leaving early. I admit I could tell that the later it became, it would not be wise to stay. That was okay. We had a wonderful time, and I made new friends.
We had an adventure.

I have had similar adventures, meeting famous people and making a few friends here and there. This is not about who's who. I am sure many of you have similar stories. The point is, some of you out there worship these people merely because they are famous. You do not even take the time to see what their message is; you worship an empty shell. You think they have it all and you want to be exactly like them. Maybe they are like my NFL friend, not happy as they are. Maybe they are like you, only a little different. In fact, I am telling you that.

They are just like you.

I keep trying to drum all of this into your heads. You do not need to be famous, you do not need a big bank account, you do not need to be so beautiful you grace magazine covers. You can be a bigger success than some of them will ever be, by merely loving yourself and acknowledging these smaller successes. You can have something they will never have— unless they change, acquire a sledgehammer and use it.

You can have a fulfilled life, with purpose.

Chapter Thirteen

You can have a message and you can teach others. You can have joy. Most people, in general, simply do not have it.

One of my friends admires Oprah, because she is one of the few who stays true to her message. She changes lives, but she is not Oprah because she is rich. She is rich because she is Oprah. Did you understand that? She is herself. Hey, she struggles. She talks about her weight and other issues. She is open and loving of herself. She seeks the truth about spirituality and her health.

Do you see what I am saying, though? She is still just *Oprah*…flaws and all…same struggles…and yet, my friend wants to think she is so very different than she is. If you must envy her, do not envy her checking account or her empire. Envy her spirit and joy. *That* is a rich message. I personally would like to erase envy and empty from your vocabulary.

Let's talk about that for a minute. **Do you feel empty?** Do you wish you had someone else's life? Someone else's looks? Let's be honest here. George?

"Yes."

Okay. Thank you for being forthcoming. I give you kudos for that. It is the first step. Since we are talking about music and Hollywood, ask yourself: "What music inspires me?

How about movies and magazines?" Ask yourself *why*. Art and music can reflect who we are. Maybe you should take a closer look at what you enjoy. It might help you find insight into who you really are. Maybe you are listening to music with an empty message. Do you feel empty? Do the magazines and movies you see, have an empty message?

Books, magazines, movies and music influence our lives. Choose wisely

Do you feel empty? Ponder that.

If what you enjoy is empty, and you feel empty, could they be an outer reflection of who you really are? Take out your magnifying glass. Look deep into the words of the songs you love, the themes of the magazines and movies. I bet each one describes how you feel.

I personally have come to the point where I cannot even look anymore. It makes me sick to read emptiness. Hey, I have to keep my level out and remain balanced. I mean, I will pick up a magazine now and then for entertainment value. I remain connected to what is being thrown out there, but I do not buy into it because I am full inside. I cannot put a void into my already filled soul, does not fit. My soul is fed

Chapter Thirteen

through positive messages and images.

Sorry, but **I do not want to be a stupid girl.** Never have and never will. I should not have said sorry...because I am not.

What are our kids seeing? If you desire these false realities to the point they make you want to be someone else, cut up your body or get Botox to erase lines, what do you think our kids feel? Hey, I did it. I cannot judge. But I did choose to realize I made a HUGE mistake. I will not become sucked into that way of thinking. I told you, I no longer allow myself to be viewed through their eyes. I have broken a pattern.

light bulb

I am not saying you should *never* have surgery or never correct something that could help re-gain your confidence. Plastic surgeons do wonderful things for people. I saw a TV special about a surgeon who provided prosthetic ears for children born without them. I was moved by the beautiful story. But when you are doing it as I did, solely to please others, and you *still* feel empty when it is done, what did you accomplish?

I am trying to tell you if you fill yourself with positive messages and eventually find your purpose, maybe, just maybe, some of those things you do not like about yourself will become something you love about yourself. You may not want to erase the lines. Those lines tell a story.

Maybe there is a story on your face you are meant to remember until the day you leave this world. If you erase it with Botox or a facelift, you will forget. Don't you see? Maybe you are supposed to remember. Maybe that "flaw" is the key to unlock the deeper meaning in your life or is the catalyst to allow the flood in and fill the void you hate so much. Have you ever stopped to think about that? Or do you just want the easy fix?

If you find the joy and purpose in your life, and there is still something you feel needs repairing, by all means search your heart and go for it. We all need improvement. But doing it because you think it is popular, like the breast implant craze, is just that—a CRAZE. CRAZY! Do you really think a man will love you because of it?

Let me tell you something, women. I walk into a room now and I am confident. Here is where you need to decide if it is confidence or arrogance. Remember? See, I love myself and people are attracted to me, both men and women. Why?

Chapter Thirteen

> Well, I know a few things.

I know there will always be a prettier woman than I am at the party, or one with a better body—always.

I know there will be a woman there with more trophies or a bigger bank account—always.

I know there will be women with degrees and more brains—always.

I know there will always be people out there who will not like me—always.

Can I change any of these truths? The answer is no, I cannot. So I accept it. But there are some things I can change.

I can promise you there doesn't have to be a woman in the room who uses her tools more than I do. No way.

No one has to be more *kind*.
More *generous*. More *grateful*. More *joyous*.
Brighter in spirit. Happier. Fuller. More *compassionate* or a *better listener*.

I can control all of these things about myself and they make me, me. That is why people would want to be around me. That is why a man might be attracted to me. I do not have to worry about the prettier girl stealing him away. Because when another, healthy-minded man sees me, he sees ME. He sees so much beauty deep inside that it radiates through my face, through my scars. She is no threat and if she tries, then she is an empty threat.

Here is where I say:

If you are healthy in mind, body and spirit, then a likeminded man will be attracted to that.

If you are empty and unhealthy, as my husbands and I were, that is what you will attract. If for some reason you attract an unhealthy man and he leaves you for the prettier girl, then you must gain more power from the experience. You must realize it is not *you* who needs to change *your* body to look like the other woman. You must gain strength in your pain and demand a higher standard the next time. Be conscious, make choices, see the red flags and you let the unhealthy man go. Tell him *he* just isn't cutting it.

You deserve a man who challenges you, not one who ogles over another woman's breasts and makes you feel you should change yours. Do not accept the one who says you cannot get fat or you need braces on your *slightly* crooked bottom teeth. Stop the madness.

Chapter Thirteen

Don't be a stupid girl. I am sorry, I am skinny. So I have a thin, athletic yoga body. No big breasts here. Sorry, guys. Guess you'll just have to get over it if you want me. That is what *you* need to be saying. Only, insert your own body part here _____.

How do we become strong? We have been learning along the way. We have some steps in place already. Let me tell you about Lindy. Do you remember being seventeen? Do you remember not loving yourself? Wanting to fit in so badly you would compromise yourself just to be accepted? Well, Lindy is seventeen and she is a typical teenager, and I adore her.

Lindy has been babysitting Caleb since he was born. I have watched her grow up. She always seemed so confident. I remember thinking she reminded me of ME. She refused to have sex, drink or do drugs. In fact, I remember her saying, "I don't want a guy. I want to go to college. Too many girls in my school are pregnant or crying over boys and they perform poorly in academics. I want to be somebody." She is. She does very well in school and she can attend just about any college she chooses.

But something happened to Lindy along the way in these last three years. She allowed herself to meet boys. She grew up and other factors in her life changed simultaneously. She somehow developed an eating disorder.

She finally told me one day, and I was in shock. I mean, she was always so skinny and different-looking, in a wonderful way. She has beautiful, flawless white skin and auburn hair. Her green eyes shine against that background. I think she is gorgeous. Trust me, when she hits about 21, she is going to make hearts ache but she does not see it yet. She felt bad about her body; she didn't like it. She thought it was flat and boring. She began to not like herself anymore. Her confidence eroded and she began to test the waters of peer pressure.

She finally did ask for help. She told her parents——a big step. Remember me and David? Or the spelling test? She did have parents she felt safe to tell and she told me, too. She had to let go of ego to let it all out. She began counseling and did receive some help, but did not feel comfortable with it. It wasn't speaking to her in the way she needed and she was having a difficult time breaking patterns.

Her friends did not understand and they abandoned her. Her boyfriend did stick by her for a time, and she relied on him as her only source of strength. He was all she had. Well, they are seventeen and you guessed it, they broke up.

I watched Lindy fade. She became skinnier and skinnier and cried often. It came to the point she could not even baby-sit

Chapter Thirteen

for a while because she cried around Caleb too much. I was so worried for her and we talked. She was trying and did not want to fall back into that trap, but what else could she do? **She was allowing herself to be seen through others' eyes and she let herself plug into a man.** Unhealthy patterns, I knew well.

One night I come home from a party, and she was watching Caleb. He had been asleep for about four hours. You know, she could have been talking to boys, watching movies, etc. Instead she logged onto my computer and discovered this book. It had not been edited and was far from being done, by any means. Guess what? I found her on my bed sobbing. She read the entire book. But this time she was not crying over a broken heart, she was crying because what she read reminded her of HER. She knew she could relate to what I was talking about. I want you to read what she told me … in her own words. …

"Sarah. I want to love myself, just how I am. I want to love my "flaws" like you do. I want to so badly. Reading your book made me think about my past. I realized if I had to write my story as you did, I knew there would be parts I couldn't remember, because I blocked them out. I blocked out the entire last year of being sick. I believed if no one found out about my eating disorder, I could get past it myself.

All I really wanted was love from my friends and family. Everyone disappeared. Brian eventually did, too. I know I need to be able to love myself, without him in my life. I believe he loved me. Soon enough, I will love me too. Me without Brian. Me without bad friends. Me without any of that. Just me … and I am going to start writing. I want to remember those painful things and try to discover the root of my poor patterns. The counselor can't help me. Maybe if I write, like you did, I can help myself. Thank you, Sarah, for writing that book."

She cried and so did I.

She has been writing and working for weeks now, and we had a talk the other night. We began to find issues and connect them to the problem, ones she never connected before. She has a long way to go, but she broke out her magnifying glass and her sledgehammer, at 17.

Are you envious? I don't blame you this time. Ironically, that is the age when the teacher told me at the formal I was too skinny, and I began a different type of eating disorder——eating too much to please others, which ruined my health.

Here I am, speaking to a girl the same age, with so many parallels to my own life. Do you think this pattern change of hers could lead to her finding her purpose in life? Like

Chapter Thirteen

mine did? Somehow I can already say YES to that. You do not need to be a psychic to see it will happen. She is changing, at 17, as I should have. My full circle is coming into light. I could not be more fulfilled by knowing she is going to bloom, and I will have played a small part in that.

You see, she is doing the work. Not me. Not her friends. Not her therapist. She is learning to write, talk out loud, locate her patterns and change them. She is picking up tools and putting them in her toolbox. HER choices. How empowering and I feel stronger because of her. God bless Miss Lindy.

You know what I am going to ask, George.

"Yes, I do. You're going to ask if that is a success. Right?"

I cannot believe you are still here, paying attention. Yes, you are correct. Is that a success? For both of us?

Lindy, you are a huge success. How conscious you are becoming and you are the prettiest girl at the party because of it. Your light is shining through that beautiful face of yours. Keep it up.

Success!

Want to hear something interesting? Lindy is going away to college and I have a new baby-sitter. Guess what her nickname is at school? "Annie-rexic." What are the odds? Still don't believe in "full circle?"

As for me? Well, I am done, I can tell you. **This book is already a success.** I do not need The New York Times to write a review and tell me it was good, for me to believe it. I do not care if they say it is bad. Someone will always dislike the things I do, always have and always will. A real writer will pick my book apart but that is not the point. My book is as successful as any book out there on the list. **I changed a life. I spoke my message. I fulfilled my purpose. I taught a child,** just as I said I would and as I was told I must. I have no fear, and these young women will benefit from it. I do not have to ever sell one copy of this to feel successful. I love this book. I love myself and I love them both.

We are all successful.

You still there? Did you learn anything? Did you make a choice to start writing and then break out your magnifying glass? Maybe take a closer look? Maybe look at all the outside sources influencing you and decide to change what you read and see? Maybe you want to love your flaws and not be in such a rush to

Chapter Thirteen

erase all the beautiful lines telling your story. Maybe you do not want amnesia. Maybe you want to remember, as Lindy is beginning to.

You can begin now.

If you have not been journaling along the way, maybe you need to take a nap and be still. Do it, here and now. Then go back to chapter one and start over. I give you permission. Seeing it on paper makes it easy to locate the problems.

Then, you can break out that sledgehammer and change the negative words to the new, positive ones. Talk to yourself out loud. Maybe you will begin to believe them. Maybe, just maybe, you will save a lot of money at the plastic surgeon's office and he will dislike you just as he is going to dislike me. We could start a club. "My Sexuals. Go ahead, don't like us. We don't care. Because

WE LOVE US and that is all that matters."

tool time with tessie

I love me! I want you to say it as Lindy now does. Loving yourself is the first step to truly loving another. Let's keep retraining our brain with our exercise, shall we?

Our tool box is getting pretty full.

Instruction manual

Screw in these words with confidence:

I LOVE MY PHYSICAL "FLAWS." THEY TELL A STORY

I know this chapter is a difficult one. Society puts so much stock in our outward appearance.

Maybe journaling will help you realize you are beautiful, just as you are. Now, draw a portrait of the "real you" and compare it to the one you drew earlier. Bet you see yourself in a whole new light.

Be Confident. Radiate.

GOD is in the Pizza

Lessons are everywhere.
Refrain from labeling others or
you might miss an important one.

Linda, is my sister's friend. They have known each other since junior high school. Linda is about 5'9" and has long, beautiful black hair and unbelievable milky white skin. She walks as if she were on a cloud. She is statuesque and reminds me of an Audrey Hepburn type. She exudes class. Anyone with two eyes can see it. She is quiet and it almost seems as if she is a mystery. She is always behaving in just the proper manner, crossed ankles, hands folded neatly on her lap. Can you picture her?

Well, one night during their college years, she was riding with her friend Chris to church. They made a pit stop to pick up his girlfriend. Linda was dressed beautifully, as always—designer suit, jacket and skirt and white blouse, heels, lovely as usual. She is always so impeccable. Well, Chris went inside to get his girlfriend and Linda decided to jump into the backseat. She wanted Chris' girl to sit up front with him, naturally.

While they were inside, she pushed the seat forward and tried to hop into the back. She lifted the lever to the seat but she could not push it forward enough to get in with grace. She tried and tried. I mean, she slammed that seat all the way up to the glove compartment, it seemed, but still could not squeeze back there gracefully. Being a tall girl was difficult enough. She realized she had to go for it, graceful or not.

Chapter Fourteen

Chris and his girlfriend were coming out, so she dove into the backseat, headfirst. Her skirt crept up her legs and her feet dangled out the side of the car. She inched her way in, straightened her hair, sat upright and pretty much pretended as if she had not been seen. Well, she was seen, and Chris and the girl were cracking up. I mean, dying laughing.

He went over to the passenger side of the car and peered in at Linda. "Have a rough time getting in, Linda?" he asked. "Oh, yes but I did it. You may have the front seat. Thank you for asking," she replied with her hands folded neatly in her lap.

He laughed—I mean, howled.

Why were they laughing so much? She was clueless.

light bulb

He walked a little farther back and opened a rear passenger door. "Linda, this is a *four-door sedan*! All you had to do was *open the back door*!"

Linda was mortified. **How did she not see that?**

We have now all heard the tale for years. She will never live it down, how a two-door hatchback magically became a four-door sedan, within minutes.

Well, that story got me thinking today. How did she miss that? Why did she? **Sometimes we have something so permanently ingrained in our brain, our two eyes do not really see what is there, right under our nose.** Does this happen to you in life? Were you raised to only believe one thing a certain way, and you cannot see it another? Do you have a closed mind? Are you afraid to see things differently? Do you label people based on these beliefs? Well, since I just happen to know many of you do, we are going to have one more little talk.

Listen, I have been right there with you. Linda will tell you I said things to her I now regret. I said them when I was young and very close minded. I also said them pre-David, with a bit of self-righteousness. Can't take them back, but I can change my thinking. **I *must* change my thinking.**

If I do not, my third eye will never see there just might be four doors when I am only seeing two. Must retrain that brain, remember? I promise I will teach you in the next chapter how we can use that blindfold. Okay?

I know you are anxious but I need to lay one last foundation. GOD.

crowbar

At the beginning of this book, I put a warning label on it and stated I would mention God. Scary! People are so afraid to mention Him nowadays and I wanted you to keep an

Chapter Fourteen

open mind to what I had to say. Remember, God is a spirit——both genders, yet neither, all at the same time. I am just using "He" so we may have this conversation. I am quite aware of the times God is a woman when speaking. Trust me, I have seen Her emotions!

> I put that warning on the book because I did not want to be labeled, merely because I was raised by a missionary family. I did not want you to assume I only looked at God in one way and was not able to see the many faces of God.
> **So many of you are looking at religion—a two-door hatchback—when you should be looking at SPIRITUALITY—a luxury, four-door sedan.**

Why are we talking about God? Well, here is the thing. This entire book has a purpose. No, I am not in a religious cult and I am not going to brainwash you into joining our commune. **The purpose of this book is to give you the ability to find the deeper meaning in your life.**

We will discuss it next but for now, we established you are trying to find your purpose, right? The deeper meaning? Well, I have to say this—and I hope I do not offend anyone—but to find the meaning, you must acknowledge some sort of power outside of yourself. I mean, if you want the superficial meaning, you have it already, correct? You are able to see the superficial meaning with your two, earthly eyes. That is quite simple, yet you continue to feel empty. You keep telling me this all along our little journey. You want the deeper meaning.

Well, going deeper means we have to use our third, spiritual eye. To use it, I have discovered you must find a spiritual lesson and connect to it. Don't you have to believe in something spiritual or higher than yourself, to see a spiritual lesson? C'mon. Do not over-intellectualize this. You know you do, even if it is simply your inner voice.

So many of you are afraid to mention God or your view of God. I understand. Our culture has brought us to the point where we are now looking at each other, religion, political views, etc., with labels.

"I don't label anyone, do I, George?" you reply in astonishment.

Wow. You are in the minority. Here, let me tell you about someone, so you can see why it is so important *not* to label.

I have a friend who sings in a band. I met him only a few months ago. What if I told you his band performs hip-hop music? You might put 100 labels on him merely because I mentioned he performs that type of music. You might have an image in your head of the entire band. You might even

Chapter Fourteen

decide you know what he looks like, what race he is, what clothes he wears or car he might drive. You might decide you will not like his music because you do not like hip-hop.

Let me tell you, Dean is a 26-year-old genius who writes brilliant lyrics. He is a white boy who happens to think hip-hop has been snuffed out by the empty messages of rap artists today. Underground hip-hop is a genre of music which gave so many African American men and women a voice, one they would not have had otherwise. He has been listening to it and attending concerts since he was a little boy. He sings his heart out about the injustice of the government, the decay of the environment and he portrays his life in his song. He looks to be about 16 years old. He has a beautiful, angelic face and I adore him.

Now, look at Dean and me for a moment. I've been called a "born-again Christian." I am registered a Republican. My parents are missionaries. Because of my ex-husband and some of my own career choices, I have the means to live in a golf and country club community. I do not drink and appear to be very straight laced.

Dean had a much different life. His father passed away when he was nine years old, and he was left at times to make a lot of choices on his own, as a teenager. Our teenage years were the complete, polar opposite. He is registered a Democrat and would definitely consider himself an agnostic, the skeptic. The word "God" is not mentioned in his lyrics, as far as I can tell. In fact, he uses a few curse words to make a point. He does not agree with the yuppie mentality and he is not afraid to tell you so.

How in the world could we possibly see eye to eye on just about everything, not only in this book, but in our lives as well? I have to say, we do not just see eye to eye, we inspire one other and we change each other's lives. We move the other to tears. Dean is my funk, soul brother, part of my soul family.

How *do* we see eye to eye? Well, people, Lucas and I do not believe in labeling. **Labels are for soup.** We believe in looking at each other and saying, "Different is good." Let us also look at what is the same. When we started looking at each other in that way——looking for the same——we discovered there was not much different. In fact, we began to notice the differences we had were positive ones and viewed them as strengths.

Dean wished he had a little more of Tessie in him: NO FEAR. But let me tell you, when he gets on that stage, all inhibitions are down and the fear disappears. He is a sight to see. He is true blue. I love to see an artist who is not manufactured. They are real and will not change for anyone. At least, that is my hope.

Chapter Fourteen

I wish I had a little more of his gift of being able to see society for what it really is. Dean can spot a phony in two seconds or less. We talk of the government, war, the environment, God and wouldn't you know it, we have similar views. He did not label me a yuppie based on the fact I live in a country club, and I did not label him as a person with an empty message *just* because he performs the type of music he performs. At first I thought hip-hop was rap music with an empty, degrading message. I did not know. But I did not close my mind and am now a huge fan of the conscious movement within this genre of music. It is so far from being empty it makes my head spin.

One weekend, he took me around Atlanta to underground, hip-hop clubs and parties. I loved it. Again, one of only a few white people, I was treated with love and respect by everyone there. No one cared about race or labels; they were there to hear the message. We were too and if we were each inspired by the same message, then we were all brothers and sisters——no race——no class based on monetary gains——no faces, and now I enjoy a new type of music just as I came to love Sigur Ros.

putty-knife

To remove labels and the strong glue holding them on

Open your mind and stop the labeling. Where did you put your crowbar?

While writing this book, he came out with his first album and I read the lyrics for the first time. You have to understand, as they are performing, I cannot hear all the words. As I read the album, I began to cry. Dean and I are the same, more than I ever imagined. His third eye was never closed. You do realize you are born with it open, don't you?

light bulb

We will get there.

He has been writing as long as he could remember, analyzing and pulling out his magnifying glass over his life, daily. He is wide awake and he sees things most people do not see. He knows his purpose for being here. He gives his message freely. Lucky him, huh? I had just finished chapter 13 when I read his lyrics. Wouldn't you know it, his album is one big summation of my entire book. I was overwhelmed by it. My book is his album and his album is my book. We could not have manufactured that.

alarm clock

To wake us up and keep our *eye* open.

Chapter Fourteen

We met only this year and he has been writing these lyrics his entire life.

So, how can we see eye to eye? **WE BOTH ONLY SEE WITH ONE EYE——OUR THIRD EYE.** That is how. It is just that simple.

Now we are able to learn from each other. Trust me, Dean is really listening to me about how acknowledging God——I mean, really acknowledging SPIRIT——how doing that can do even greater things in his life. See, he has been stung by religion as many of you have been. Maybe you see things in the churches that make your heart break. Good. I am glad they make your heart break, mine too. That is why I am telling you to take the word RELIGION and stick it in a shredder. Hey, do not freak out, "religious people." I want you to throw it in the shredder and replace it with a new word: SPIRITUALITY.

Religion has evolved over the years and not always for the better. We can all see that now. I wish it hadn't, trust me. If I had said this years ago, I would have been shot. But now, it is happening everywhere and what I am saying is being accepted.

One of the last churches to which my father could relate, had a huge scandal hit this year. The pastor was jailed for molesting young girls and my father wept for days as it broke his spirit. If it did not break anyone else's in the church and they are still sitting there, comfortable on their little pew, shame on them. But it is not my place to judge. I can only look at myself and my family. We will not be a part of such utter disdain of the purpose God originally designed the church. That is why we are in the highways and byways. Seems to be the only place we can stomach it anymore.

I enjoyed a book last night by a brilliant, and I mean brilliant, man. He talks about spirituality as I do and is hilarious. I laughed the whole way through and was amazed at how much we have in common. I think I want to stalk him and attend his church. Of course that would mean I have to commute from Florida to Portland, Oregon every Sunday. Dagnabit.

I purchased about 20 copies of this book and have given them to my friends. You would not believe the response when they read it.

I receive notes and letters telling me how it renewed a passion inside them for what spirituality really is. They thought it was dead. It is not; it is very much alive. Simply look around you.

Chapter Fourteen

Are you awake? Do you want to wake up?

Hey, I have atheists as friends. Can you believe that? Even they believe in something bigger than themselves. One of my atheist friends loves Mother Earth. I say, great, let's look at the *same* in that thought and relate, and we do. For the first time in his life, he felt he could talk to God. Awesome. I learned more about Mother Earth and have become more "green." Even if he would not have felt that belief towards God, I would not have minded. I am happy simply in our friendship and the fact we can talk, open each other's minds and not be blinded by labels.

What if I was sitting on my little, comfy pew looking down at everyone who did not attend *my* church? At everyone who did not believe exactly as I do? Judging them because they put curse words in their music and get drunk now and then at a party? Oh, they must be going to hell, I should say. What if I was like that, labeling everything and everyone around me?

Well, a lot of people do it. That is why my saying I am a Christian has gotten me labeled—and not in a good way. I dislike I am labeled like that. Of course, when people get to know me, they do not think it anymore. But still, I dislike it. Labels.

What *if* I behaved like that? I would be miserable, first off. Secondly, I would be living in a world of nonsense. Thirdly, I would not have these wonderful friends around me who teach me so much, and I teach them. Don't you see? That is why Jesus was hanging out in the highways and byways. He was teaching. I am telling you, I would have been stalking Him. We should all be teaching, relating and finding out what is the same.

I like to imagine Jesus had an internal monologue that went something like this:

"Look at these people. They appear empty and lost. I want to reach them, but we do not have much in common. We have different religious upbringings, race and class.

What do we have in common? Let's see. Think, Jesus, think!

Oh! I know! We are all hungry. That is a start. Well, I suppose I will just sit down here and eat with them. This one common thread will bring them closer to understanding me and what I can offer them. I will be a beacon of light at this dinner table. Let's eat!"

Chapter Fourteen

I read so much of Him eating with people, simply eating. He saw that thread of commonality, took it from there and He was smashed for it by the "religious" people. "Eating with sinners." Go back and read it. It is interesting.

"Please do not write me letters about how I should not have written a monologue. I intend no disrespect to my Jesus. You have to understand, we kinda talk like that to each other. I promise," I plead.

So, I am not here to tell you to become a Christian. On the contrary, I am just asking you to relate. It is that simple. I do not align myself to any one religion. My friends have to relate to who I am just as I must relate to what they believe. It is necessary it work both ways if we are to see eye to eye. We do it and I am the better for it. Hopefully, so are they.

If you want to wear the bracelet that says WWJD (What Would Jesus Do?), you better understand what He would *actually* do. You better break out your Bible and really start reading. Not with your two eyes, but with your spiritual one. I will not wear one. I am sorry, you can get mad at me, but I simply do not like to *sell* Jesus. It is my little pet peeve. Each of us is entitled to one. I am sure I have touched yours in this book.

I want to switch gears and tell you a little story. One night, my friend Tom was drinking a little too much, and was with a group of friends. He was full of life and talkative as usual, and they became very hungry. Tom likes to talk about God at these times and he looked at the pizza in front of him, as he hugged each of his friends while proclaiming, **"God is in the pizza! Look, guys, God is in the pizza!"**

Everyone laughed and they still tease him when we go out. "God is in the pizza, Tom." Ha-ha-ha-ha-ha-ha-ha.

Now, I do want to say one thing real quick about him. Due to family illness and other situations in his life, he has made a choice to change his pattern of drinking. Remember my grandfather and the strokes? Well, Tom has decided he does not want a "wake-up call" to knock him on his you-know-what. I admire him for it. He is breaking a pattern, as are other members of his family. My dad and granddad did, too. I give them all kudos.

light bulb

He took out his sledgehammer and I took mine to my man pattern. Is his pattern more "sinful" than mine? Is mine more "sinful" than his? No. **Quit labeling and categorizing even our poor, unhealthy patterns.** We must both create new, healthy ones in their place and I, for one, am glad we are in each in other's lives to keep it all in check. It is nice to have someone who can challenge

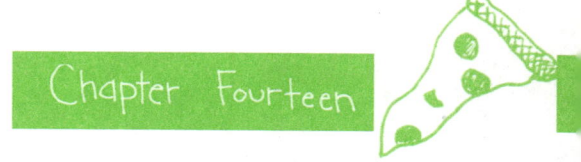

Chapter Fourteen

me without being a nag. There is a big difference.

As I was writing this book, I began to see all the patterns in my life. You are seeing them too, right? I hope you have been journaling and are seeing the patterns in your own. Well, when I began to see the intricate design of my life, I knew there were no accidents. None. Everything did happen for an ultimate purpose and I began to see God in everything that happened to me thus far. Remember, you can substitute your word here. You need to, because I want you to really get this part of the book. Change God into what you need to in order to relate, okay? Do it now.

I began to think. **Is God in everything?** I asked myself that very question and I looked around my house with my spiritual eye. Not my two eyes, my third one. I was amazed. I saw Him in everything, even my son's books, movies and his video games. Everything! These were not spiritual movies or books, just regular books. I saw God in my movie collection, in magnets on my refrigerator … in just about everything I focused on.

Then Caleb wanted a piece of pizza. He put a slice on a round plate and it looked like this.

Then he took another slice, put it on top of another and that looked like this. ...

Now look at what he did with the pepperoni. ...

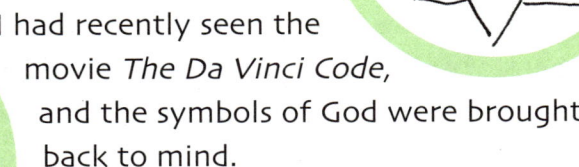

I had recently seen the movie *The Da Vinci Code*, and the symbols of God were brought back to mind.

I said out loud, "God is in the pizza!"

Tom was not around, but I wanted to tell him I loved his drunken rant. God really is in the pizza! He is in everything. Did you notice the pizza made the Star of David—a symbol of God? The whole pattern was the basics to the Flower of Life, an ancient symbol used to explain our very existence. Amazing. I know it may seem silly to you but I am telling you, when you use your third eye you can see EVERYTHING differently. You can see the luxury, four-door sedan right under your very nose.

Your higher power is in everything. Your inner voice. Mother Earth. We are all connected. We are one.

Chapter Fourteen

Your life is one big, beautiful, intricate design. Even the bad things you think have hurt you, were there for a wonderful reason. Why don't you take a moment to look at them with a magnifying glass and see how it happened for your ultimate good? Turn that negative into a positive. C'mon. Do it for me? If I can, you can.

I need you to connect to this idea: There is a powerful force trying to shed light on your purpose for being here. You can find it and you no longer need to wander aimlessly through life feeling empty inside, wishing you could discover it. It is right there under your nose. Maybe if you keep journaling and writing, you will see it. I want to help you see it ON PAPER, like a formula that cannot be disproved.
Are you ready? Because,

We are finally here!

Time to get out the toolbox and put on that blindfold. We are going to build something special with our third eye—not our two earthly eyes. I am going to ask you to blindfold the two "working eyes" and force the brain to open that third one! You ready? You just might find your purpose for living and I want you to be prepared.

Be careful what you wish for.

I found mine and I now have a big task to undertake. I cannot be afraid. Be prepared to take out your mop and broom. Fear and worry need to be swept off of every step we build.

I will warn you, there will be a shift in the way I teach in the next chapter. I want you to understand, as I analyzed my life and discovered my reason for being here, I realized I formulated a guide to teach you how to do it as well. I would like to share that guide with you now.

Remember, take out your pen and paper, because **I will be instructing you in how to create your own blueprint to build a staircase.**

I will offer suggestions, but you will be the one actually doing the work.

Chapter Fourteen

Be prepared to work.

It is fun, remember?

tool time with tessie

I love talking about God and I am not afraid to do it. You should not be either. I hope you will send me letters about your views so I may continue to grow. For now, let's do our exercise.

We needed an alarm clock to keep us awake. I also like using mine to remind me of my lunch breaks. Drop the "label remover" in the box, as well.

alarm clock

putty-knife

Screw in these wonderful, simple words:

I AM AWAKE!

Do you feel as if you are still sleeping?
Do not be hard on yourself.

Keep working in your journal. Open your mind and see God in your life; you will be glad you did. Put a few affirmations on your refrigerator for all to see.

Be Awake. See.

Stairway to Heaven

Do not attempt to find your purpose by walking in the footsteps of someone else's life. Walk in your own.

My sister and I had a friend in high school named Anthony. He was crazy. I mean, a real nut job, but very funny. We all loved him. I always thought he should be on stage somewhere. Well, Anthony loved to be the center of attention and he made no secret he was trying to get it. We could be walking along, minding our own business, and he would race by and hurl himself down the flight of stairs directly in front of us. Just hurl his entire body down the stairs and try and knock any observers over like bowling pins. There would be no warning; he would run by like a flash of lightning and do it. He was nuts. We would laugh, and of course he relished in the attention. I thought about him today. I know he watched *Saturday Night Live* and admired Chevy Chase, the master of hurling himself down stairs. Anthony achieved the same effect, by imitating his idol. Imitation is the sincerest form of flattery, right?

"Where is she going with this, George? I'm ready for her to tell me what my purpose is," I hear you saying.

Okay, okay! We are ready to talk. Breathe. So, you want to know why you are here on this earth? You think maybe my book can help you? So many books out there are inspiring and wonderful. You read about people finding their purpose after having a life-threatening disease, and they woke up. There are those who made a fortune and now want to tell you how they did it. They want you to follow in their footsteps so you can achieve the same goal.

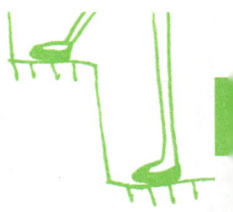

Chapter Fifteen

Well, while I love reading these stories and become inspired, I have one problem. I do not want you to climb their steps. That is the path which led them to their purpose. **I want you to build your own staircase** to lead you to yours. I wish you to find it and I do not want you to be like Anthony, falling down a flight of stairs you were not meant to climb in the first place.

Here we go...

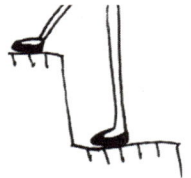

Step One: Overview

Ambition
Let's break this down to make it easier to understand, shall we? I must tell you, this chapter has been known to overwhelm a few people. Do not be discouraged if it does and do not be in a rush. Take the time to be still and hear. You may take as many breaks as you wish and absorb.

I like to look at it like this. **What is the purpose of my birth? Who am I?** The age-old question. You are you, is my answer. You have a purpose and a message and I cannot have you falling into the trap of thinking your message is my message, or the one of the pretty, famous lady on TV. You might discover they are the same, and I say great, but you must do the work to find out.

I know, you want an easy fix. Don't we all? We already established society feeds us that lie. In my experience, easy doesn't fix much. It appears to for the short term, but definitely not the long one.

Let's suppose you want to climb the steps, reach the top and discover your purpose. It is up there waiting for you. It is simple, you must build the staircase first, then you can climb it. But be careful, we do not want a dangerous path, do we? I do not want you to fall down a flight of stairs. Building an entire staircase can be overwhelming, so let's begin with just one step. I need our tools to build the pattern that will get me to the top. The step is the pattern. The pattern is the step. Become accustomed to saying that.

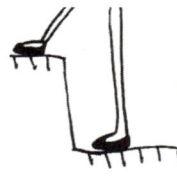

Step Two: Choose a plan

Decision

Answer the question: **Do I want a solid, safe staircase or do I want a rickety, hole-ridden, dangerous one?** If I want a solid staircase to lead me to a solid message and purpose, I will make wise choices. I will build each step with care, set healthy patterns in place and repeat this process until it is built. I mean, once I get up there and find what I am looking for, I can make more choices on what I will do with it.

Chapter Fifteen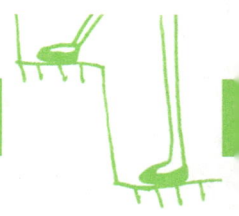

Who knows what I will build then, the sky is the limit. By building something as simple as a flight of stairs, we will have the principles in place to fashion something even greater. I cannot tell you what to build but what I can promise, you will know how to use your tools. The choices are up to you. This is a journey to <u>personal</u> empowerment, remember?

On the other hand, if I did not take my time, was not conscious about what I was doing, and rushed through building each step and setting each pattern, my staircase would not be solid. The patterns would be negative ones. It might be dangerous. It might hurt me. I might fall down that flight of stairs over and over and never reach the top. Or worse, if I somehow got up there, maybe my message would be an empty one and I would have no skills to erect something bigger and greater than just a rickety ole staircase. I would believe I had something important to tell, but it is merely this empty thing no one wants or needs to hear.

I would stay stuck there, not knowing anything more than when I started. I would become an endless cycle of repeating the same mistakes over and over and not getting anywhere. Sound familiar? Do you ever feel that way?

Do you have the visual?
As an example, let us take a look at a famous, rich person you admire:

I am speaking of one you can clearly see is not living a conscious life. He may seem rich in the world's eyes and claim to have found his passion and purpose, but he walks a rickety, negative path full of holes. I can promise you he has an empty purpose and an even emptier message. The void inside consumes him as he tries to fill it with women, toys, drinking, parties, more toys, bigger toys, etc.—you get the picture. Living for money is his purpose. What a sad message. So, be wise, my friends. You may make it to the top, but what will you give the world or your children? I, for one, want to hand them something they can tell the next generation and the next. What about you? Or do you want to be like this famous person? Rich yet empty.

Step Three: Demolition

Inspiration
Now the good news. Let us suppose you have already built a rickety, dangerous staircase and you are climbing it. You know who you are.

Chapter Fifteen

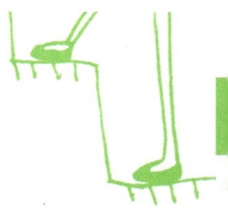

You are sitting there saying, "Dagnabit. I keep sliding down that flight of stairs, George."

Let's take a lunch break as we formulate our plan of attack. Find your motivation to change, the inspiration. Maybe you only need to tear down one step, one pattern. Perhaps you will merely grab the crowbar and pry off a piece of rotted wood, then make a choice to replace it with a fresh one. Maybe you need to demolish the entire staircase and you will require help. That is okay, do not panic. I will help you right now. You and I can take out our sledgehammers, rip it apart and throw the refuse in our trashcan.

"I wonder if I should have given some of you a wrecking ball in place of your sledgehammer. We could really have some fun with that!" I cry as I rub my hands together in excitement.

Tearing it down is the first step. Not so overwhelming, is it? Not when you do it one at a time. Lamp, not spotlight, remember? Remain in the *now*.

Step Four: Locate tools

Organization

I will keep walking you through the building process. You too, George. Have you been journaling or at least been locating tools for your own toolbox as we have been moving along here? If you haven't, you need to go back and see where you acquired these tools or if you even have them at all. Sometimes it is easy enough just to know you possess one, other times you need to take out the magnifying glass and find them.

I personally have been collecting tools along the way, and I put them in my tool *shed*! My box was too full! Point is, I first had to accept them; knowing they are there is not enough. I have to go one further and use them. It is my choice to pick which ones and when I use them. I may not need them all at one time. Got that? Make sense? YOU make the choice.

Some of these tools may be handed to you by your parents, some you may stumble upon. Others may be harder to find, like the hidden picture game where all the tools are hidden in the bigger picture. Remember that game as a kid? Some you may have to purchase, such as buying a book or using a counselor. The point is, find them.

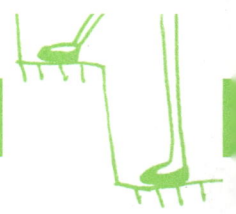

Chapter Fifteen

Here is a visual to help you locate a tool and find a lesson.

1. I want you to take a story in your own life and write it down using your two eyes. Draw with the visualization of a horizontal line. Find the story in your life, let's say, that taught you about being different, like my patch. Write it down and in your mind, imagine it is written in one long straight line, like this:

2. Now, to find the spiritual lesson, we must locate the story using our third eye. Remember? Put on your blindfold and reach into your spirit. Listen to your inner voice. Talk to God. Feel Mother Earth. Allow Spirit to whisper in your ear. We have established we must use the third eye, use the word "spiritual lesson" and acknowledge something other than yourself to find it. Pull that magnifying glass out and put it up to your newly opened eye. Draw the parallel line like this:

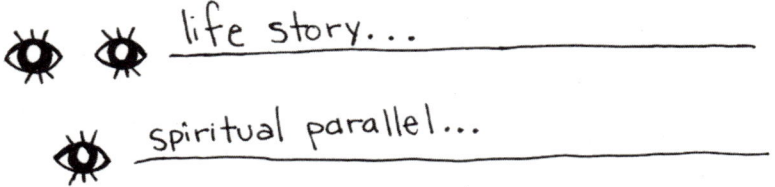

Did you find a lesson? If you did, you can move forward. Write the lesson under the second parallel line.

3. Ask yourself, "What tool did I find in this lesson?" You may use my stories as an example or find a new tool. I encourage you to find your own and put it in your box.

4. If you did not find a lesson or tool, do not be discouraged. Keep writing. Keep asking, *why*. Why did this happen? How did it benefit me? How did it hurt me? When has something like this happened before in my life? Are they connected? What can I now do to change my attitude about this experience? Or what can I do to keep this pattern a healthy one? Ask the simple questions:
Who? What? Why?
When? Where? How?

Trust me. These questions make all the difference. Even if you have a negative feeling about the story you wrote, keep working until you choose to see how it worked for your good.

why? where? what? when? who? how?

**You will locate the tools.
I promise.**

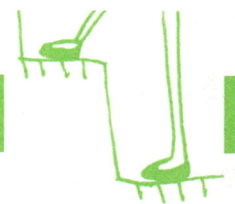

Chapter Fifteen

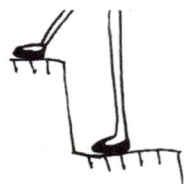

Step Five: Build

Expansion

Now that we have the positive lesson, let's build our first step. Keep finding the parallels when you see it again and again in your life. Find them all, spend the time and write.

Begin to see how these lessons created a pattern.

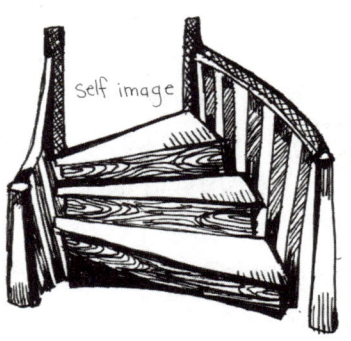

Self image

Name your pattern.
Example: Self-Image.
You now have a blueprint.

Preparation

Switch on your light and cover the light bulb. We do not want anyone knocking our light out. I mean, I want you to shine. Seal off the work area with caution tape and put on your hard hat to protect your mind. We cannot have others come along and disturb us as we work, or discourage us with negativity.

CAUTION! CAUTION!

I personally like to turn up my music and find inspiration as I work. The right type of music can also drown out the ones standing outside the caution tape, waiting for you to slip up. Oh, yeah, they are there. Trust me. They sit there like mosquitoes waiting to suck your energy. Shoo! Here, borrow my bug spray. I still had a bit left over from Mexico.

Let's take our time to review the instruction manuals and handbooks we have chosen. Did we choose wisely? Take one last look at your blueprint and have the pen handy to make changes when needed. Be flexible.

Are we ready to begin with a healthy, positive attitude? Choose a few paint colors to reflect your attitude or mood.

Some of you will prefer a simple wood stain. Nice. Have them ready for a bit of fun later.

Chapter Fifteen

Directions

Take out our wood, "choice," and measure it. Is there a label stuck to it, almost impossible to remove? That glue can be a bear.

Take out the "label remover" and scrape it off. We might even need to strip residue from our choices. That putty knife sure is handy, huh?

Next, decide if you want to use the circular saw to cut a limited edition design into your pattern. Put on your protective goggles as the doctor instructed. We want to protect that third eye. We only have one, remember?

Grab the level to be sure we are balanced as we begin the next step to the process.

Pick up your positive power drill, strap on your confidence-drill bit and locate a screw. Let's drill the screw into the wood as we say, **"I love me, just as I am."**

 Use our wood glue to secure it with belief as we proclaim, **"I am different and different is good. I love my "flaws;" they tell a wonderful story."**

Say it out loud. Pick up more screws. Speak those positive affirmations aloud for every life story you include in our pattern. Carefully screw one in at a time. If someone slips under the caution tape, shakes your confidence and loosens a screw, do not panic. Re-group and find your screwdriver of  reassurance. Tighten the screw as you repeat your affirmation. Let my mother chase them down with the bug spray! She was the champion, remember?

Inspection

Fill any holes that may have been poked into the wood by negative-termites, with your bondo. Get that putty knife and smooth your surface.

Chapter Fifteen

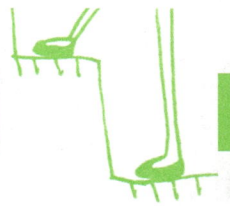

"Ah, Bondo…Cow Pie…you are missed." Sorry, my mind wandered there for a bit.

Are you sweating? Great. That means you are working. Seal the step with our stain or paint it, if you like. We need to protect it from the rot and decay of filthy, negative thoughts.

Protection from the outside elements is essential.

How do you feel? Pick a color and allow inspiration to guide you.

Once it dries, check it for cleanliness. Sweep fear away. Do not let it seep into your step, into your pattern.

You love yourself now, just as you are. You are not afraid you will slip back into hating your "flaws" again. As you sweep and mop, shout, **"I erase fear and it feels great!" FEAR IS THE NEW F WORD!**

Keep the broom out for when others try to blow it back your way; we know they will try. Know you secured it with belief and it is safe to climb.

BE STILL

"Wow! I am feeling empowered just by standing up here!" you exclaim.

Standing in your own power is a feeling words cannot describe. Chills is the best word I can use. Sounds simple, but you do not know what my chills feel like!

It is now time for our break. I hear the alarm sounding. Lunch time! Rest. Be still and hear. Does a new pattern come to mind? Do you need to grab the pen and add to, or revise your blueprint? All of these choices are yours. Do you feel empowered?

"I do!" shouts George.

Good for you, George. I am really beginning to see positive changes in you. We are getting somewhere. Take as long of a break as you need. Do not rush.

Chapter Fifteen

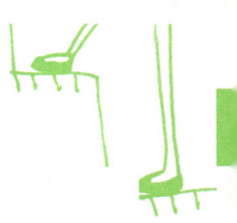

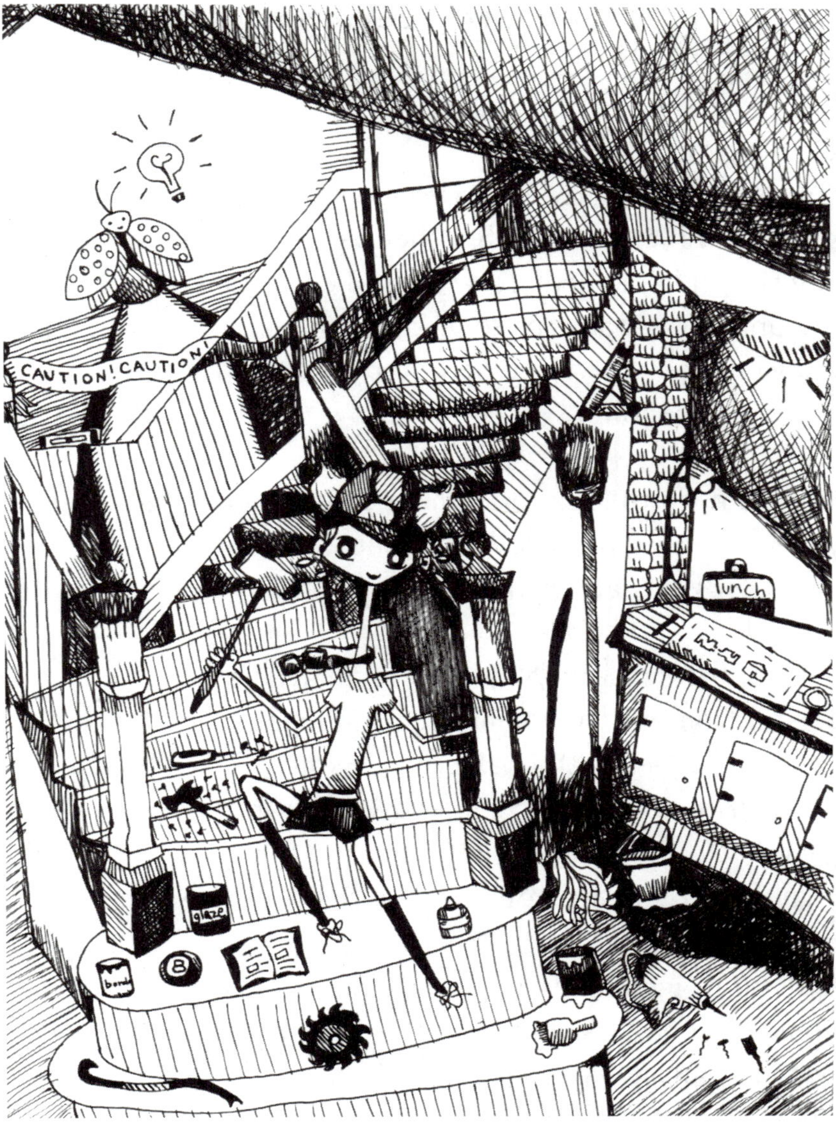
CAUTION! CAUTION!
lunch
glaze
bond

Stand on your new step and be proud!

Step Six: Seeking help

Compassion

On to the next pattern. Do you need to use the sledgehammer to break another pattern? Okay, no big deal. Say this, "No big deal. It is fun and exciting. I do not want my unhealthy patterns to lead to poor choices any longer. I have already built one new step and it is not scary. It is not overwhelming."

Do you need to look for someone healthy minded to help you? How will you know if he/she is healthy?
Okay, let's talk about that.

Take out the magnifying glass to analyze the person from whom you are seeking help. Can you see a healthy pattern in his/her life? Write down what you know about the person. Do they make wise choices in their own life? If you are not sure, ask them.

Are you trying a new form of therapy or exercise, as I did? (Reiki or yoga.) Ask yourself: Do the principles they teach provide tools for me? Did those lessons line up with what I am learning to be a healthy pattern? If the answer is *yes*, then by all means, use these helpers. If the answer is no, or you are unsure, wait until it becomes more clear.

Chapter Fifteen

Do not choose someone who will accidentally forget to secure the step or distract you with negativity and cause you to forget. Make sense? It can be a process. Do not be afraid to use your patience-drill bit, and please keep that third eye open. Set the alarm clock to keep you awake if need be.

Allow me to say something else to you. **When you are having a struggle in your life, do not confide in those you know are unhealthy.** You already know they will discourage you and gossip. Why do that to yourself? If you have no one around you consider to be healthy minded, maybe you should distance yourself from your friends for a little while. Maybe the only person you can confide is God or your journal. That is more than fine. Do it and begin to change. I can guarantee, **as you change, you will discover who your true friends really are.** Take it from Tessie. I happen to know this first hand.

Step Seven: Connect the steps

Introspection
We keep tearing down and rebuilding. Keep setting one healthy pattern on top of another, one by one. Look, a staircase is being formed. I am excited! As we connect the patterns, we screw in a light bulb along the wall. We will not look ahead. We merely turn on one light and see what we can see, then build. When we have an "ah-ha" moment, we screw another one in until we reach the top. Easy breezy.

"Did she say 'easy breezy'?"

Yes, yes I did. You making fun? Hey, don't forget your light cover!

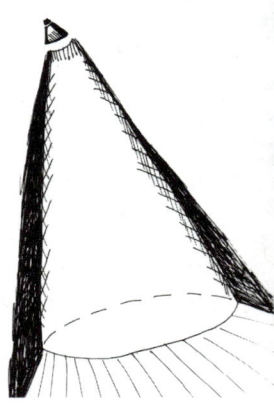

You might need to turn on the spot light now and then, when you need the "bigger picture" to expand your blueprint. If it becomes overwhelming, turn it out and get back to your lamp. More choices you will need to make.

The point to all of this is I am telling you, with authority, you must begin to write. You must see some of this on paper. As you practice, you will not need to write it all out;

Chapter Fifteen

it will become a habit. I understand I am repeating a few points here, but you must **write the positive messages and then say them out loud,** until they *become* habits. Habits become patterns, remember? It all begins from ONE thought. Some things bear repeating. I mean, do you keep *repeating* the same mistakes? Since we already established you do, I must repeat the steps and become your antidote. Make sense?

Hey, this will take time. You cannot expect it to happen overnight. You must now take the quiet time to go inside yourself and connect the dots. Some of you will build a staircase quickly and others will take much longer. Maybe you will need more naps or more assistance. Maybe you began reading this book having no tools at all. It is okay, do not be hard on yourself and begin from square one.

It will happen for you, if you do not quit the potato sack race. Maybe this will be the first time you do not give up on something. Great! You will acquire the perseverance-drill bit while writing. Amazing. **Write me and tell me about it.** I would love to show George. I suggest another nap before step eight.

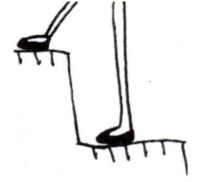

Step Eight: Climb

Realization

Time to climb our solid, safe staircase. What is up there? You want me to tell you?

"You just built a staircase to a platform of your own, personal train station!" I exclaim.

"George, she lost me. I didn't expect a train. This girl kinda drives me nuts!" you say as you throw up your hands.

Leave George alone. He has an open mind by now and he likes trains, just as Caleb does. He knew I would never mention trains in this book unless I was planning on talking about them.

A train station. YOUR CHOICE. You can stand up there and be a healthy person if you prefer. Live up there and have a nice life, and you will or you can choose to board the train——the circle of life——and allow these lessons to travel with you. We can run over and over these lessons along the way, until they become deeper. Here, I will help you understand what this train can do for you.

Let's put on our blindfold and use me as an example:

Chapter Fifteen

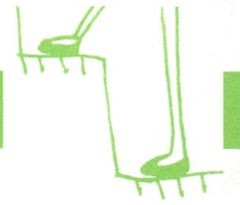

Use your newly opened third eye. Every time we talked about the patch, the meaning became deeper, didn't it? You know it did. We went from cute ladybugs on my patch and a contact on my other eye… to scars and make-up… to finding my purpose… to the patch actually retraining my brain to open my third eye. There was no contact lens on the third eye; I pretty much put a telescope on it instead.

Lastly, I handed you a blindfold to begin the retraining of your brain, just like Pirate Patch Sarah Bear. This brings us back to the beginning. Full circle. Pretty deep stuff. Stuff someone else may have never connected… not with their two eyes, at least.

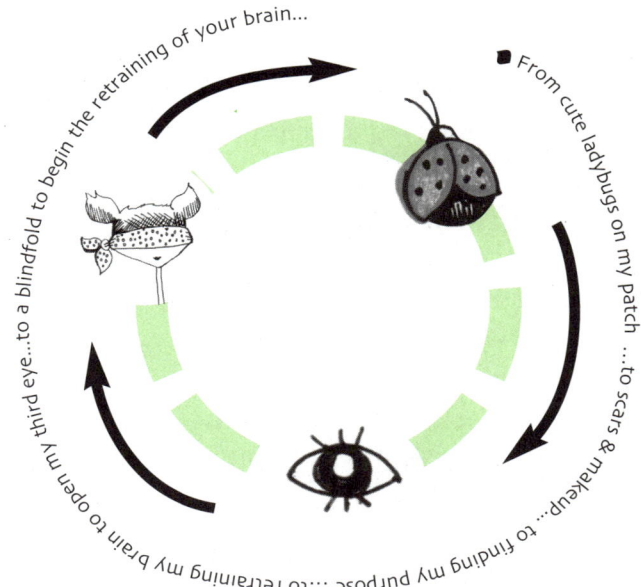

Let us take another example of a lesson that came full circle:

REPORT CARD	
LESSON	Grade
The spelling test I was afraid to tell my mom.	F
David and the abuse. Afraid of him. Afraid to tell my mom.	F
Spilled tea. Afraid of my mom.	F
Derek and our marriage. Afraid to tell anyone.	F
Caleb and the spilled juice. Afraid to tell me.	F

It came back to the beginning. Simple little lessons, led to much bigger ones. You will begin to notice this principle in your patterns. Connect them and see how the meanings become deeper, until they come full circle and are simple, yet again… back to the beginning.

Chapter Fifteen

Step Nine: Find the deeper meaning

Completion
If every time we go over and over these patterns, and they become deeper and deeper, we find the *deeper meaning*. Right? If we can do that with just one pattern, can we not do that with our entire life? YES! We can look at the life, up until now, and find the deeper meaning!

"George, she really is saying she has the answer to the deeper meaning of life! I mean, she is really saying it out loud," you say in disbelief.

"By George, I think you've got it!" I say with satisfaction. C'mon, admit it. You're having fun.... Silence. George? Silence. He is a tough one, but I am winning him over. I hope I am winning you over, too.

So, why a train? Simple, a train track is a circle.

Connect
Here, look at this. **We want to find the lessons and have them come full circle**, right? Let's take the parallel lines we drew earlier and do this——connect them——choose to connect the superficial and spiritual meanings together like this:

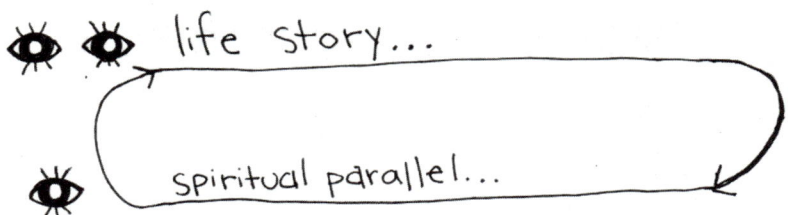

Now we have a circle and we may take this lesson and run over it, until it becomes deeper and deeper. But unless we connect the two meanings, we cannot go over them again, and you would continue on an endless straight line. Some would tell me a straight line will eventually become a circle if you write long enough. I agree, but how long will that take? You could be dead by the time it does and I for one, want to know why I am here, while I am HERE!

You must connect them, people. Drill that into your head. I like to look at it as a circle. Perfect. Infinite. The circle of life. God is a circle. The alpha and omega. Beginning and end. Use the train track. Jump aboard and as it goes round and round, it will come through the station and find a deeper meaning. Then keep going...

Blind eye. Patch. Contact lens. Mountain. Station.

Chapter Fifteen

Someone else's eyes. Scars. Make-up. Valley. Station.

Life purpose is found. Beautiful field. Station.

Blind third eye. Patch. Telescope. Tunnel. Station.

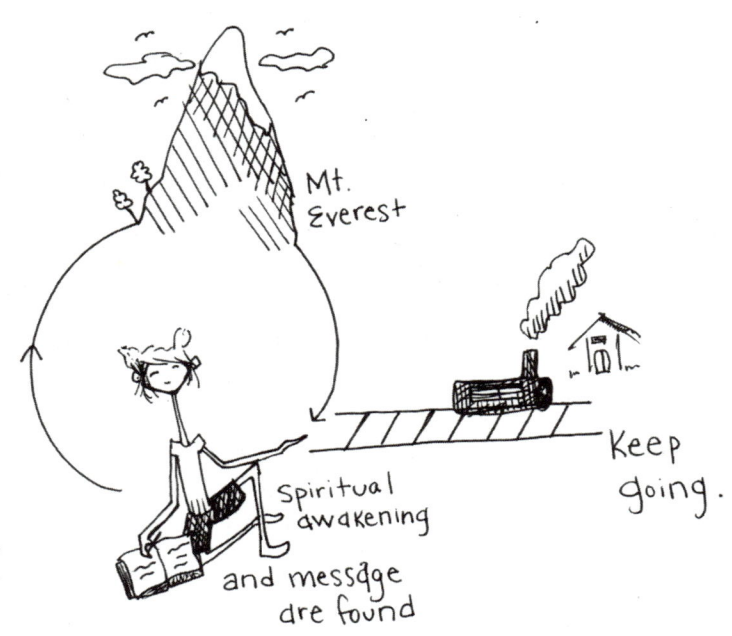

Spiritual awakening and message are found. Mount Everest. Station.

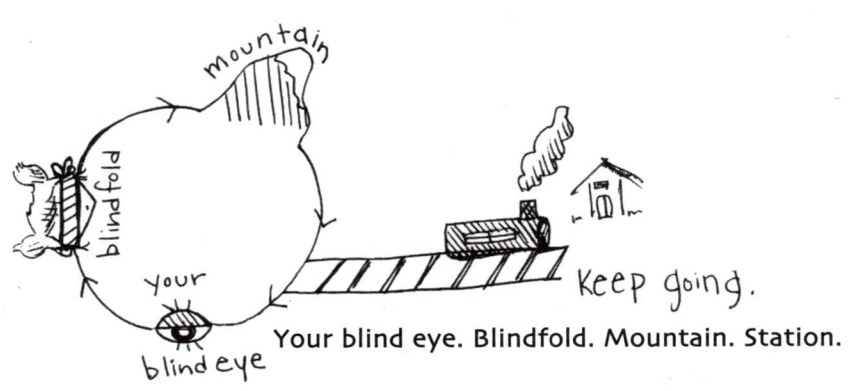

Your blind eye. Blindfold. Mountain. Station.

Chapter Fifteen

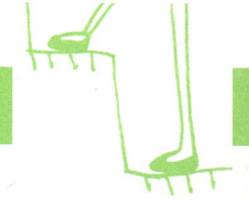

Now, you keep going. Find your valley, beautiful field, tunnel and then climb Mount Everest.

Hop aboard!

It is now time for you to make a choice. You may hop aboard and let yourself go up and down the mountains and valleys of life with a new eye, and travel through the dark tunnels to find a new lesson.

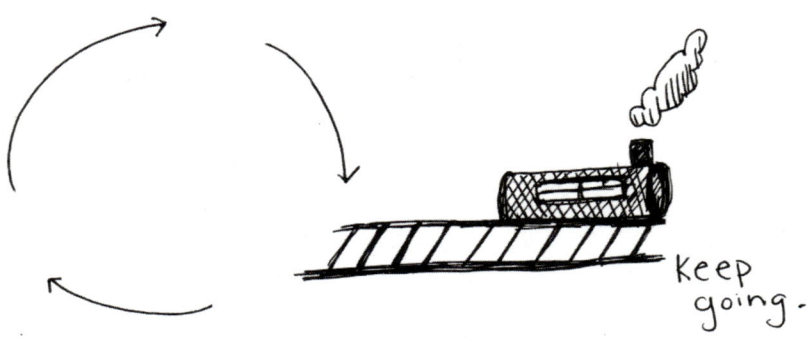

When you reach the station each time, you will see the deeper meaning and the dots will begin to connect. Your brain will be retrained to force your third eye to see at all times, trust me. If you do this, your blindfold will become a permanent fixture upon your face.

I love my patch.
May I never take it off.

Chapter Fifteen

Analyze

Once you see how each event came full circle, draw a circle and label it. i.e. Patch.

Label them all until your paper is full of circles. As you analyze your work, you will want to go one step further and connect them to each other. You should have seen my journal. Circles everywhere!

Want to simply find the deeper meaning to life?

Allow me to explain what happened to me. I let my mind go, in circles… round and round. I joined each lesson to another.

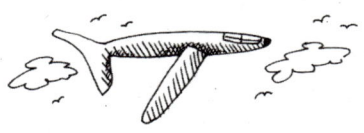

Eventually, the train was not fast enough and I climbed a new set of steps, to an airport terminal. I boarded a jet and rode around in it for a while.

I raced around the globe until I finally climbed my last set of steps, to a launching pad. I boarded that rocket ship with a loudly beating heart and
I have never been the same.

Not only did I find my purpose, I had a spiritual awakening—the most special moment of my life. It became my inspiration for writing this book, for moving forward with no fear. Something that to this day is difficult to put into words, and I am tearing up as I write. A special seven days, which I am able to fully share with only a handful of people.

In a way, it is a lonely feeling but not in the way you define "loneliness." I simply mean very few understand my experience and therefore, friends have fallen away. But I feel more empowered by God than I ever have, yet at the same time, feel smaller than a grain of sand buried 10 miles beneath the deepest ocean floor. I believe that is true humility, but I am not a philosopher. I can only tell you what God told me in those days, and in the days following. I will never forget seeing His "face," and I do not want to. Do you see now why maybe my own, imperfect face seems trivial?

But I chose to board the train, the jet, the rocket ship. I was not afraid and I allowed myself to do the work. I connected the circles and let them build upon each other, and I was not afraid to acknowledge God. All the paths led to the same place. My purpose was in writing, on paper. My message became crystal clear and you think I am nuts, don't you? Don't answer that.

Chapter Fifteen

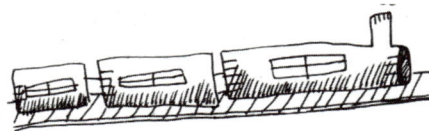

Go only as far as you feel comfortable. My atheist friend loves Mother Earth and he is happy on the train. I wanted to see God, so I boarded the rocket ship. We both found our purpose, our message. We are both fulfilled. But I must point something out to you, I have the privilege of reaching outer space because of my choices. I am not bound by the gravitational pull of this earth. **The boundaries of your freedom are for you to discover.**

For me, when I say I stand in my own power, I mean Source empowered me and I chose to acknowledge it. Humanists will disagree with me, but I want to share what personal empowerment means to me. You need not agree to apply the principles, remember that. Your choice.

"Man, she says CHOICE a lot. I am getting her point."

FINALLY. Thank you, George.

That is the key.

It is your CHOICE. Train, jet, or rocket ship?

Step Ten: Keep writing. Keep working.

Intention

I am asking you to begin seeing the deeper meaning in everything. Practice, practice, practice.

Keep asking: WHY? WHAT? WHERE? WHEN? WHO? HOW?

Isn't that what we are taught as young children? Caleb asks *why* all day long. I will never tell him to stop, as most parents do. He is born with his third eye open. It will not close if he keeps asking *why*.

When did you stop asking *why*? Did your parents become annoyed? Did your teacher? Did your pastor? Why don't you start doing it again, as little Caleb does? Drive everyone crazy by asking, WHY!

Start from the beginning. I told you I had to do that in the introduction. Now do you see why I did it? Even the Bible

Chapter Fifteen

starts with "in the beginning." This book is a circle. We began with the patch and we are ending with it. I had one eye in Chapter One and I now only want to use one eye, my third one. You are all exactly like me, born with one eye open. You did not realize you only had one eye when you were imagining me with my patch on, did you? Stop cheating and looking under your patch. It will never work if you do!

Listen, I know it sounds a little out of reach, but it isn't. It is actually the most simple thing you can do. Write. You have known how your entire life. Look at Dean's. He began to analyze and he wrote lyrics for as long as he can remember. He never stopped writing, and he found his purpose. He even has a song entitled *Keep Writing*. The proof is on paper. If we have not convinced you, let me tell you about Mannie. Mannie Billig.

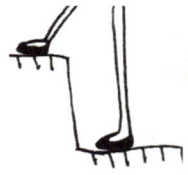

Step Eleven: Teach

Illumination

A few months back, I ran into a man named Mannie when I was at a spiritual center. A mutual acquaintance introduced us and we talked for a bit about my wellness center, only ten minutes. He encouraged me and told me he understood my passion. He owned his own business, but I could tell he loved to talk about Spirit. He ended up giving me a little book he wrote, which he signed. I did not think of him again.

Well, I have to say I was going through my divorce, and he sounded too positive for me. I did not want to read Mannie's book; I wasn't in the mood. I wanted to pout a little. You ever feel that way? Wanting a pity party? Anyway, I left the book on my kitchen counter for eight months. Never even opened it, until this week.

I was cleaning the kitchen and the title caught my eye. *The Art of Falling in Love With Your Time on Earth. A True Story.* I opened it and began to read. I did not get very far when my eyes began to well up. His book was my book. My book was his book, just like Dean and his album. His chapter entitled "Choices" was the same as Chapter Ten, "Don't Throw Darts." He had one called "Finding Your Purpose," "The Awakening," etc. He told stories, wrote his life story, and asked the reader to do the same. I was amazed. He had an awakening and wanted to tell the world. He wished to teach others and desired that everyone find their purpose. He was content to hand out his little love letter of a book. I knew he and I would be able to talk for hours.

I found his business card in that book and called him. He eventually remembered me and we did speak for hours. We

Chapter Fifteen

were energized, inspired. We are going to talk again. He has plans for a wellness center and maybe we can join forces. I will give you a web address where you can order his book. Send me letters. I will publish some on the site. Maybe you will write a book and we can sell it for you. Someone will want to read how you found your purpose, I would. Everyone can be like Tessie. BE TESSIE. We are all writers and we all proceed without the "F" word…now.

Maybe you will be the only one who reads your book. Great! We are all the same, but different. You and me. Mannie and me. Mannie and Dean and me. Marie, the massage therapist. Anne, the yoga instructor. My parents, the list goes on.

We are all wide awake and our stories are the same. We each found our purpose; different ones, but the same message. Amazing. Miraculous. We are all proclaiming it loudly for the entire world to hear. **Why not you?**

Every day, every situation, every negative thought. All of it … life … it is all YOUR choice.

Learn to become a conscious person.

Stop reacting to everything happening to you and stop building your patterns without thinking.

Quit leaving your tools in the toolbox. Slow down, be still.

Think.

Hear.

Learn.

Build healthy patterns that will carry you through life; patterns that will produce a healthy message people need to hear, want to hear... teach the children.

Let's break these patterns together and teach them.

DEAL?!

Because no matter who you are, where you come from or what you have become now, I think we have established the fact we do not see our youth learning healthy patterns from Hollywood and the magazines, etc. Let's teach them not to give their God-given power away. Let's teach them how to build a stairway to heaven—a heaven on earth. Can you imagine? I will if you will.

Chapter Fifteen

"Well, I am the odd ball. I have an 11 step program, not 12 like most. Sigh. Different is good, right?" I say as I shrug my shoulders. 11 seems to be my number.

I also want you to know one last thing. Because I do not want you thinking they are the only steps out there, I am hesitant to even put the 11 steps in print. Create your own blueprint, this was merely mine.

"I am sure you can do it more efficiently, George. Here's to hoping you do.

Salud!"

tool time with tessie

Do you need to take a nap before we exercise? I understand and encourage you to give yourself permission. Chapter 15 was a lot to take in.

In this chapter, we were able to finally use our tools to build, but this does not mean we should stop looking and growing.

I hope you are journaling to locate more screws. I would not want you to forget they are there. Here is mine:

FINDING MY PURPOSE IS MY GREATEST SUCCESS

Be Enlightened. Grow.

Tessie Strikes Back

Sometimes you must say you can do something, before you ever try. Success is in the eye of the beholder.

Now we need to get back to my purpose, right? I mean, that is the point. George, you coming along this time?

"Yes, ma'am. We are friends now, you know that. Don't make me say it twice."

"I won't. I'm in shock you said it once," I reply.

The Apartment Showcase

Well, I am back to being 20 years old. Remember I told you I was working in the apartment industry? I applied for the job as manager of a 200-unit luxury development. I would be the youngest manager in the company by far and would be managing about six employees. I did not like working for a previous manager, thought she was kind of lazy. I wanted to make a difference and a few improvements, so I decide to go for the interview.

Brenda and I hit it off right away. She asked me a million questions. I had never been a manager before but I sold her on my abilities. I had been in Mexico and was not up to speed with computer programs. She asked if I knew how to create intricate Excel spreadsheets. I said, "Sure, I can do anything." I got the job, and immediately went to Barnes & Noble to buy a book called *Excel for DUMMIES*. Sound familiar? Tap shoes?

Success!

Chapter Sixteen

I loved that job. For being only 20, I was making a lot of money had a free apartment with a garage. The apartments were luxurious, and many NFL Jaguar football players lived there during their first years with the team. I told you about one of them and I became acquainted with more. I kept their identities hidden and they loved me, all my residents did.

Well, except one crabby old lady named Mrs. Kravitz— you know, from Bewitched? Okay, so I named her that. She was always so nosey and a pain to deal with, but there is always one. She gave us years of entertainment. If she was so miserable, why didn't she move? Anyway, I loved the residents, even Mrs. Kravitz. I loved my job. I did learn to create Excel spreadsheets, by the way. By now I am sure you already knew I would. Tap dancing— my version of "fake it till you make it."

One day, these guys approached me with a marketing plan for the apartment industry in general. The Real Estate Channel was popular on cable, and they wanted to make commercials for the apartments, purchase time on that channel and make a half-hour show out of it. They were cameramen with no sales skills, no abilities to write scripts and they were without any money. Good idea, but if you cannot sell one ad, you are sunk.

Guess who knew how to sell ads? Remember Tessie and Duffy with the Annie programs? Sure, I could. I took over pretty quickly and quit my job. It was not too difficult to sell ads when you knew every apartment manager in town.

Here is where I say, never burn a bridge. I am not perfect, but I was taught that lesson and am glad I listened. Because when I needed to go out there and sell these ads, I am so glad I had not ruined my relationship with any managers in town. You never know, keep those bridges intact. Trust me, I have had to suck it up and swallow my pride many a time—but it is worth it. I stand firmly behind this truth and I cannot say it any more simply than I just did, so I will leave it at that.

These camera guys were cool for a while. They taught me a lot about the process, but they wore on me. I used all of my own money and borrowed some from my dad. You all know he did not have much. I wrote all the scripts, did the voiceovers on some of the commercials, worked with the editor, directed and found people to be in the commercials. I had become the producer, writer, and director within weeks. I was saying, "White balance this scene," and I did not even know why I was saying it. Sound familiar? Always the tap dancing.

Success!

"George, this girl is nuts. How does she get herself into these situations?" you ask.

Chapter Sixteen

I know, I am nuts. Never said I wasn't.

There are vendors who work very closely with these apartment communities, such as carpet cleaning companies, etc., and they wanted to sponsor the show we were producing, now called "Apartment Showcase." We made commercials for them, too. I owned the business by now and was working until 2:00 a.m. writing these lil 30-second scripts. Exhaustion was a regular thing.

My camera guys began showing up late and eventually missed days altogether. My sister Shavaun was married now and her husband, Edward, was a cameraman. How convenient; I had to hire him. That was hard, because these guys started this, but they would not take responsibility and we were falling behind. They partied a lot as I wore myself out. Do you see what happened? It is not enough to have a good idea. You must have a strong work ethic to succeed. You must serve others, define new lines, take responsibility for your commitments, sacrifice your own desires and put your own money on the line. Do you see where I had all these tools in my toolbox by now? Those camera guys chose not to pull theirs out. I am not sure they ever acquired some of them. Are you beginning to see how these tools can be used for everything you do in your life? I hope so. Remember this one thing—different is good, but when it comes to business partners, it's a whole new ballgame. Choose wisely my friend. Choose wisely.

Well, since I am nuts, I decided we should be doing this in West Palm Beach, too. My sister Alison lived there, and wouldn't you know it? She was working for the apartment industry there and knew just about every manager from Palm Beach to Boca Raton. How convenient. Tessie and Duffy are reunited.

We hired two other salespeople and we rocked out the commercials for almost two years. That was a success. I had three full-time employees, plus the camera guys. We lived like that with me owning my own business. It was fun, tiring, and we were proud. I was only 23 years old.

Success!

Unfortunately for us, the Internet boomed and apartments would rather spend their money on ads there. I understand. It is cheaper and everyone shops online now for houses, apartments, everything. Time to pack it in. I paid my dad back every dime. I only had about $5,000 on my credit cards left to pay, not too bad. I decided to go out there and start over. I took a test and obtained my real estate license. I knew I could never go back to working for someone else again. I had enjoyed my freedom too much, and we all know I was not afraid.

The Wonderful World of Real Estate

They were advertising for real estate jobs at World Golf Village. I love golf, so I applied. My interview lasted about five minutes. When the guy left the room, I thought he

Chapter Sixteen

hated me until another guy came back. Apparently the first guy did like me in those five minutes; said I was spunky. I was offered a job selling timeshares. I was told I would only work about 25 hours a week and would make a six-figure income. They were a reputable company, Starwood Hotels. They own the Westin, Sheraton and W chains.

Just 25 hours? Technically, I would have to work *for* someone, but with all the extra time I could formulate another business, right? Cool. I took the job. When he handed me my instructions for where I was to report for training, I asked, "By the way, what *is* a timeshare?" He laughed. His name was Derek. I had just met my future ex-husband.

Here I am taking a job and did not have a clue as to what I would be selling, just knew I could do it. Tessie was now my alter ego. I mean, she never left me. I went to training and decided if I did not like what I would be selling, I could quit. Turns out the company is amazing and their timeshares are really wonderful. I even bought one for myself. I did make the money they told me I would. I was a success. The people I sold to, loved me and I loved them. It was fun, and I was happy.

Success!

Derek and I began dating. He moved on to the company he works for now. He made it big and I knew he would. People told him he was crazy for leaving. We did not know if his

new company was going to make it or not.
I encouraged him and told him, "Hey, if it doesn't work out, then come back here. No big deal. It's only money. You can always make more. What is the worst that can happen?"

Well, he was the ninth employee and now there are well over 1,500. The company did take hold and he shot up in rank fast. He was loyal and I was proud.

Are you afraid to step out of a job causing you misery? Do you know your passion or purpose, and are afraid to go for it? If you know you have the tools to "make it" and yet hold onto fear, then you are selling yourself short.

Go ahead, ask yourself right now, "What is the worst that could happen?"

Write it down. Say it out loud. I dare you. Say what the worst thing that could happen is. Maybe it is not so terrible. Maybe if you talk with your spouse, you may be shocked to find he or she will support your crazy scheme. My dad did. Derek did. Why not? What is the worst that could happen?

Professional Volunteer Mom

Anyway, we were married soon after. It was a fun first few years. I ended up quitting the job. A new company was taking over the timeshare complex, and I did not like them. Starwood was solid, but the new one was not. I could not

Chapter Sixteen

figure out what I wanted to do, so I became a full-time volunteer for the Florida School for the Deaf and the Blind.

These kids live there and I wanted to raise money for them. They are unbelievable. Talk about living without fear. I joined the staff as a volunteer and helped promote golf tournaments, etc., to raise funds. It came easy to me. It was just like selling, only I did not get paid, the school did. I felt rewarded and I was full. I mean, Derek was doing well and we did not need my income. I was not greedy. I enjoyed the time I gave. It made me feel whole.

Success!

I had become my mother. Volunteering and helping others was fulfilling. I now have a complete understanding of why she was happy all the time.

Then we had Caleb. Our marriage went downhill after that. Derek was traveling and I was basically a single mom. You cannot keep a relationship alive like that. Well, the rest is history and here I was, five years later, without a job, separated and scared. How was I gonna do this? I loved staying home with Caleb. I did not want to work full-time. I decided fear does not control me, never has. I quickly swept it away with my broom and mop, sealed it, secured it with belief and began to use my creative, circular saw.

Be

In those years of my doing volunteer work, you already know I found my passion, my purpose. I told you we would get back to it. The health stuff was what I loved. I become a wellness coach. I did not have paying clients, but I was helping all my friends and family with diet and yoga tips. I enjoyed teaching others to find their connection in mind, body and spirit.

My dad had become ill, and my parents were already discovering alternative methods for healing and eating. Our lives were becoming one again. I was being drawn back to them with health. I loved it. Derek thought I was a freak. He hated it. He let Caleb and me eat that way, but he would not. He made fun of me and I was not supported in my beliefs. I tried to suppress it, but I just couldn't.

Right before we separated, I woke up one night and God told me to build a wellness center. It was to have a natural spa, yoga, martial arts, organic café and juice bar, life coaching, acupuncturists, health food store, nutritional counseling, and a resource center. I even had the idea to have a place to put your children while you used these services. They could be learning in a fun environment, too. Everyone asked, "Sarah, have you ever developed a piece of commercial property before or built a building? Have you ever owned your own business?"

Chapter Sixteen

Well, I had owned Apartment Showcase, but I had never developed a commercial piece of property and I certainly had never overseen a building being built. We had not even built our home. But, hey, I am Tessie, remember? So, sure, let's do it. I bought an acre and a quarter and developed it.

Success!

"George, why am I not surprised," you say, shaking your head.

You shouldn't be.

I learned so much. I had to win over the city planning guys. No problem. People love me, remember? They are so cool and I love them, too. I had to win over the surrounding residents. People do not like developers, apparently. They ended up loving me, too and vice versa.

Success!

I learned the process to design my building with a company called Florez and Florez. The owner, Rob, built me up and encouraged me. I was humbled by his gifts and willingness to help. He did not have to. Most owners hand off the project to someone else once the account is secured, not Rob. I honestly believe he would do just about anything to help me succeed.

Success!

I found an engineer and a land planner. Man, that is a job. I have a new respect for all these guys. I tell them so. Don't worry, I tell them thank-you. I had a new respect for Derek, but he does not develop one and a quarter acres, he develops small cities.

What is happening now? I started it and honestly, it is a three million dollar project. I am divorced now and am trying to form a partnership to put it all back together. I had been afraid to go ahead with it alone, but then I remembered my mom. She would not allow the lack of money to stop her from her purpose. Neither did my dad, remember? I have to climb that step. I have no excuses.

Tessie, the Tap Dancing Author

So, here I am, writing this book. This is the biggest tap dancing lesson of them all. I have never written anything except those 30-second commercial spots. I have to say I have never had more fun doing anything in my life. *I Can Tap Dance* has given me fulfillment. I cry, I laugh, I inspire myself, I jump up and down and talk to myself! It is a blast.

I was inspired to sweep all fear off my staircase, and just let people read what I write. I experienced my awakening and God reinforced my inspiration. He is the one who handed me the sledgehammer! So I did it. I wrote the majority of this book in seven days. Seven days! I mean, I had to fill in spots and refine it, but the heart of the book was done in

Chapter Sixteen

Success!

that precious, short time. What a feeling of accomplishment.

I now have two children's books which will be coming out as well. They also teach these lessons, but in a fun way for the younger ones. Tessie and George are the stars and they somehow end up on a train. Wouldn't you know?! We need to start them early, right? Teaching our children. Isn't that what I am telling you to do? I am screaming it! Also, I have joined forces with a social worker and we have 11 books in the making. We are determined to assist single parent families as they cope with the difficulties they face. The *Monkey in the Middle* series is giving us great fulfillment.

Even though this is not actually "building" my center, I am staying true to my message, aren't I? I am helping people in their mind, body and spirit by doing all these things. I know my books will sell as needed and the money will come. It has to, because this is my purpose. I am not in fear. These books will help to "build" the center, but it may take longer than I thought.

"Patience, Sarah," George says with a smug look.

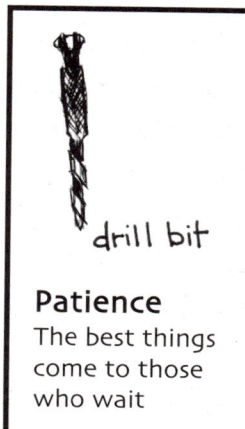

drill bit

Patience
The best things come to those who wait

Oh, you couldn't wait to throw that back in my face, could you, George?

I have decided to use a not-for-profit organization to handle some of this. My parents made me a board member of theirs years ago. How convenient. I want to use them so we can offer scholarships to those who cannot afford these services. Trust me, people who use the services and can afford it, will donate. People who are into the natural way of doing things are kind and generous. I watch them do it already. They help others in my yoga class, at restaurants, etc. I see it all the time. We believe in full circle. What goes around comes around. Reap what you sow. I will donate money. I always do. You cannot sit out there and tell me you do not have the money to get help.

Be On-line

Our website is already a blueprint for the actual center. You can access all these resources right online. I promote several healthy ideas and products for becoming the weight you are born to be. I have anti-aging products which are natural and give you energy at the same time. Organic recipes are available. The journals we encourage you to use are there and healing aides are in the "making."

We want to help you find resources to all these services in your area and the books we have been talking about. Mannie's book and my dad's album are available. We

Chapter Sixteen

developed our own clothing label, *Be Yourself*. We have it all. I cannot tell you how many fun products we are developing. And teens, go check out our *Teen Scene*.

All the tools you need are there. We provide links to other tools as well. Maybe you need help in a crisis for eating disorders, abuse, etc. We can point you in the right direction or provide books to get you started. There are free hotlines to get help in many areas.

This all is a success. I am living out my passion and purpose in my career, without fear. My message is being heard. I am not afraid to tell it. I am promoting others who do the same. Some people never have one day when they step outside the box and speak their message.
Most have not even found theirs. My theory is, they are only using their two earthly eyes. So, I am a success already, right now—— today. I told you about Lindy, who has heard my message and is waking up as we speak.

As I said, I could have written this book when I am 80 years old. Then I would be able to tell you about the huge successes I have enjoyed and all the lives I have changed. But remember, I do not believe you need an empire to be a success.

I also feel you can relate to me more now, than if I was a

household name. You may read stories and say, "Yeah, but she is famous. What are my odds of being another one of her?" Now, that is where you are not listening. You are going to find your purpose, not hers or mine. **You are a success!** Are you really starting to see that now? I hope so; otherwise I am going to have to get after you with my positive power drill! I have now received education in the alternative health field. See why conventional schooling would have been a waste?

Go back and thumb through this book. Count the success ribbons. I personally gave up the count at 40.

Keep dancing

So, people, listen up. The small successes you find will lead to bigger ones. I was setting myself up for this entire process during the course of my life. I erased fear on the smaller projects, and now the bigger one does not seem overwhelming. When my thoughts become too vast, I come back to the lamp. I turn out the spotlight and take it one step at a time, staying true to my purpose.

The spotlight was turned on this past month. One acre and a quarter may not do the job for the center. I know I need more space. Uh-oh, that means money. Well, tell your friends to buy my book. He-he. Seriously, if God showed me I can develop one acre, then how hard can it be to develop 10 times that or 100 times that? Point is, I have no fear. I am ready. Bring it on.

Chapter Sixteen

Success is in the *eye of the beholder* and the eye of this beholder says I am successful. I say YOU ARE SUCCESSFUL. Using your third eye is so much more fun. I am happy and I am having a blast spreading my message. I hope you have heard it loud and clear. I hope you will visit our website and say hello.

Maybe you can meet my cool mom. Or George. Ooohhhh … or John's leprechaun.

I hope you will write me and let me publish your story in our website's BE TESSIE section.

I want to hear your successes and share them with the world.

I want to hear if you have woken up.

We all want to congratulate you.

I want to hear how you cried when you brought out your sledgehammer.

Dean cried when he heard I was telling all of you to write. It brings joy to him. Let's make him sob! Write, people. Tell me how you love your flaws now. Tell me how you love yourself just as you are. Let us know when you find your purpose or decide to board that train. I will even give you a little discount on our products if you tell me a story and I print it. How about that? You can be a famous writer.

Tell me your ideas. Together we can change the world and maybe "Imagine" will not just be a song anymore. Imagine that. George and I are starting a club and we are going to help people. Wanna be a member?

As for me and Dean, if a "born-again Christian" entrepreneur and a liberal, agnostic Hip-Hop artist can join hands, anything is possible.

Chapter Sixteen

Next stop, world peace.

tool time with tessie

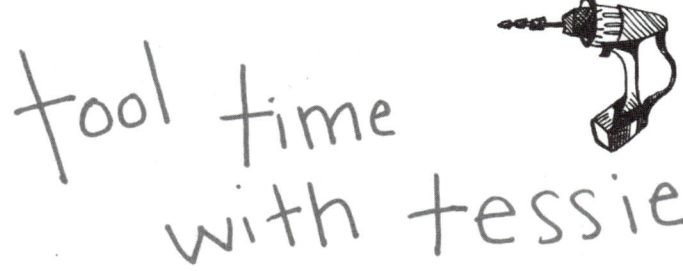

When you finally find your purpose and begin speaking your message, you may find you need patience as you wait to reap your reward. I know I do, but I just keep moving along, working.
Exercise with me.

We put one more
drill bit into the tool box.

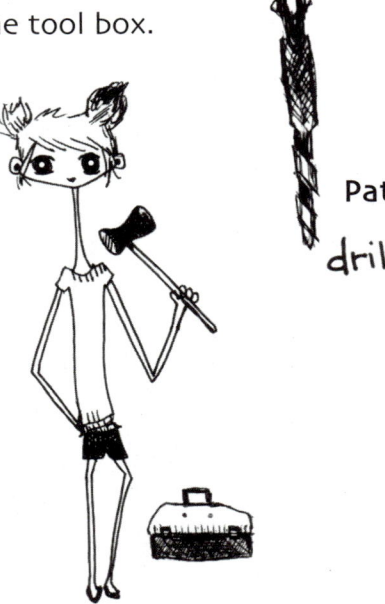

Patience
drill bit

Your screw for the day is:

   **I AM A HUGE SUCCESS!**

I believe and then achieve! I now teach others how to see that "screw" in their lives. If you do not believe it for yourself, how can you reach another? **Journal a success story of your own.**

Be Rewarded. Teach.

Hasta Luego

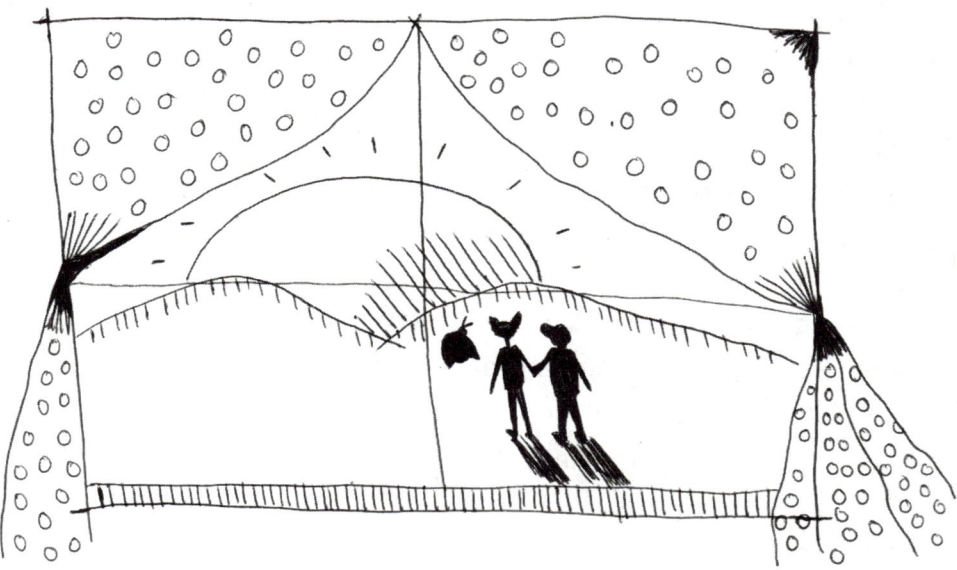

We are not saying goodbye, just "see ya later"…

I was eight months pregnant when Bogey was hit by a car. It was horrible. The UPS man comes every week to the front door and leaves my packages, along with a treat for him. It was the Christmas season and he had so many packages, he made several trips to his truck. Bogey followed him, tail wagging.

He was safe in our front yard—until he saw a squirrel across the street and made a mad dash for it. Before we knew it, a car hit him and like a flash, he was back in our home. Blood was everywhere and the stench was unbearable. I had never smelled that smell before: the smell a dog emits when he is terrified. Whew. I was shaking and crying. Bogey was bleeding pretty badly. We rushed him to the vet and he spent several days at the animal hospital. It was horrible. To see him hit, killed me inside. And if that killed me, how would I feel when my child-to-be was injured?

But Bogey did come home, with scars, just like me. Scars. You can already see the lesson, I am sure. Boundaries. Remember I told you there are no fences in our neighborhood and how Bogey wandered into Bill's yard? Well, he was safe inside the boundaries of our yard, right? Never got into trouble, never hurt. But as soon as he stepped out of them, he was run over. He had never defined for himself what those boundaries even were. With no fences being present, there was no one there to define them for him, and now he was injured. The scars remind

Chapter Seventeen

him and all of us what can happen when boundaries are not set. Remember that. **Some boundaries are not obvious, but oh, how important they are!**

I point it out at the end of the book because this is where I am in my life. I am building my new "relationship step" and learning how important healthy boundaries are, not only with men, but also those people I allow into my life. In fact, I am learning HOW to decide which people I will even allow in. **I am putting up healthy boundaries.**

Men and others are not running over me any longer. It is a process. I am not an expert in this area by any means. My parents are assisting me on this one, as they build a banister on my staircase of life. I bet you think I forgot about explaining what the hammer and nails were for when we built our staircase, huh?

Well, I told you they were for our helpers. They are forming a banister for security, something to hold on to. They are helping us create boundaries, helping us in so many ways as we climb that staircase. They are our safety net. I am so grateful for all the people in my life who build that banister for me. **I am glad I learned how to make sure only healthy people are woven into my safety net.** That is key. Because if unhealthy people are woven into that net, well, it will not be very strong and you just might fall straight through, the next time you fall. Doesn't sound very intelligent, does it?

A friend pointed something out to me the other day. She said I often put myself on the back burner while others live out their dreams at my expense. Sometimes I give *too* much and I am learning when enough is enough. Maybe I did that because being on the front burner would mean I would have to be a leader. Maybe **I wasn't living up to my full potential** and therefore **not fulfilling my entire purpose.** Maybe I was afraid no one would follow or that being in the spotlight of the world would mean I would be scrutinized. There's that "F" word again.

Funny thing is, when I recognized this and connected to it, I stepped up. People began to follow. They asked me to lead and recognized I was destined to. I realized yes, I would be scrutinized, but that is okay. I have learned not all people will like me, and I am human. I screw up, obviously, but that doesn't mean I cannot learn from it and teach others. I have found strength in that. I promise to keep you all in the loop on what is happening with my new pattern and what I learn from boundary-setting.

I love it. I love my life. I love the potholes. I love the sunshine and I especially love the rain.

Chapter Seventeen

Now, here we are. George and I. We are writing as we sun ourselves next to this refreshing pool. Do you wish you were here? We do. We are people-watching. I love doing that, remember? Watching and observing is a hobby of mine now.

We see a man here by our pool. His name is Brad. His three sons are running all over him. No one is listening to one word Brad says. They are doing cannonballs near people who are trying to relax, yelling and running. Everyone around them is annoyed. He looks exhausted. His wife is nagging him for not paying attention to her and her needs. His phone is ringing. He answers it. One of his sons wants to try diving for the first time. Brad tells him he is not big enough and does not assist him. The boy cries and wails. More people become annoyed. Poor Brad. He is just one big unhealthy pattern just waiting to be broken, isn't he?

Tessie says to George, "George, I have my trusty Magic 8-Ball right here. Let's pull it out and ask it if we should go help Brad."

Yes, I have a Magic 8-Ball. It is a lot of fun and it makes me laugh. Leave me alone.

"What? You have a Magic 8-Ball? Can you even buy one of those anymore? You are truly nuts. NUTS! We are supposed to be making choices instead of leaving our lives up to chance, remember? Using that is nothing more than throwing darts," he replies, dumbfounded.

"Wow. You really were listening and learning George, and now you are creating new habits by making choices. I'm proud of you. I bet all the folks reading this book are, too. Okay, then, what do we do?"

"It is obvious we must help him and give him a toolbox. He needs a few tools, also. May take a while, though. I will if you will," George retorts.

"Bring it on," Tessie says.

Tessie and George. George and Tessie. Can you picture it?

Hey. You! Yeah, you… the one reading this book. While George isn't looking, wanna shake the Magic 8-Ball with me? It's kinda fun. I know we are not supposed to because we are making choices, but maybe just this once? For a laugh?

"Yes! But let's hurry before he finds out," you whisper. Okay. Here goes …

QUESTION
Should we chase down Brad and help him?

Chapter Seventeen

ANSWER
Without a Doubt!

"Well, there you go—confirmation. Don't look at me like that. Gimme a break. I still like to be silly now and then," I say.

We can all take ourselves too seriously sometimes. Finding the deeper meaning to life does not have to be boring and *so serious*. Loosen up a little. Be a kid. Have fun and while George and Tessie rush off to chase Brad into the sunset—smile and laugh. **Write. Take a nap.** Please, because you know they will be back.

Somehow I get the feeling this whole "boundaries" thing will open up a whole other can of worms. There are many more lessons out there. I do not think they could fit into one little book. You did not think I thought I discovered all of them, did you?

Oh, they will be back, you can bank on it. They are tap dancing and the music hasn't stopped yet. I hope it never does.

Hasta luego…
Until we meet again…
Keep writing.
Keep dancing.

Be Tessie.

tool time with tessie

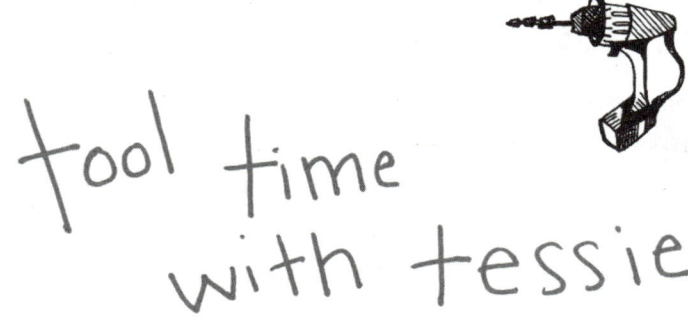

I am sad to leave you, but I will be back. If you turn to page 387 of this book, you will find a web site and I am there. George and a few new friends are with me.

We found one last piece of the puzzle——the banister.

*To all of you who build the
banister on my staircase of life, I
thank you. Words cannot capture what
you have done for me. I give you my heart
and allow you to enter into my inner circle.
I appreciate the safety net you have woven
for me and thank you for preventing
me from falling into the well.*

Be Tessie.
Create.
Succeed. Shine.
Live. Feel.
Hear.
Give.
Love.
Survive.
Change.
Act.
Connect.
Radiate. See.
Grow. Teach.

To you, the reader.

Thank you for allowing me to share and I pray you took something with you from our journey. Knowing I touched a life is my paycheck, so please write. I will be waiting.

xo

To my one-of-a kind family——
I love you all and thank you for traveling this path with me.

I would like to end with a special dedication to Caleb. I am humbled by your insights and proud you chose me as your mother. You tell me you are a teacher, and I am honored to be your student...

All my love

Remember...

We are not saying goodbye, just "see ya later"...

Be in touch!

www.justbeopen.com
is the be website

Visit our website to contact Tessie, find journals, CDs, books, clothes and lots more!

Be inspired and open your mind.

READ.books
WRITE.journals, etc
WEAR.clothing
HEAR.cd's
SEE.dvd's
IMAGINE.art
REJUVINATE.spa products
SUPPLEMENT.health products
FOCUS.yoga products
INDULGE.jewelry and accessories
PLAY.children's products and toys

be YOURSELF

i can tap dance

is a collaborative effort

Sarah R. Ulmer
The Dancer

Pictured with her mother

Sarah resides in St. Augustine, Florida, with her three year old son, Caleb. Her mission is to heal the mind, body and spirit. She is the author of *The Wise Train* children's books and co-author of the upcoming *Monkey in the Middle* series, devoted to assisting children as they cope in a single parent environment. Look for her *I Can Tap Dance* workshops in a city near you.

Down to earth people, beaches, yoga and avocados make Sarah smile.

Lisa Conn
The Illustrator

the creator & illustrator of The Adventures of Tulip-Milk-Bread is a recent college graduate who enjoys playing with her cat, Finnegan, & imagining & drawing the creatures that seem to grow inside her brain. Her favorite place in the world is Rome, Italy (and she wishes she was there now drinking cappuccino's... which she also enjoys, very much.) Her current project is learning to play her old German accordian and continuing her career as an artist.

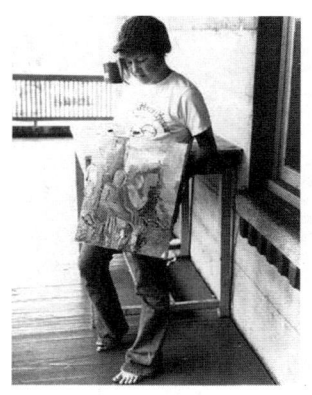

Jody Marcil
The Designer

Jody has been designing her whole life—— graphics, clothing, interiors... the be logo and now, this delightful book.

She lives with her husband and children in St. Augustine, Florida.

Jody is in the process of launching a clothing line for the *be* label.

Coming Soon!

The  Series

The children's Bill of Rights in a single-parenting environment.
By Jontie Hays LCSW and Tessie
Illustrated by Lisa Conn

and...

The Adventures of Tulip-Milk-Bread:

When your heart goes somewhere, your body has no choice but to follow.

By Lisa Conn